The Tyranny of Talent

How it compels and limits athletic achievement... and why you should ignore it

Joe Baker

aberrant
press

Baker, Joe

The tyranny of talent - How it compels and limits athletic achievement… and why you should ignore it

ISBN: 9781738644100 (Print) 9781738644117 (e-book).

Dedication

With heartfelt gratitude and appreciation, this book is dedicated to the undergraduate, graduate, and post-doctoral students I have been fortunate enough to work with on this research.

Contents

Introduction

I've always been fascinated by the notion of talent, perhaps because I never thought I had any. I was an average student through most of my time in primary and secondary school, and although I had a bit more success later in my educational journey, I defy anyone to find early indicators of it in my childhood or adolescence. In sport, I was a better-than-middling athlete, first in triathlon and then endurance running, although again, there were no indicators of any future competence in my early sports experience.

In fact, the evidence suggested something else entirely. During my childhood in the 1970s, all Canadian public-school students were required to be part of a national evaluation (the Canada Fitness Award Program) and although it was intended to promote health and physical activity in Canadian youth (it didn't really, as reflected in rising rates of inactivity, obesity, and diabetes in that decade and the decades since), it also provided feedback to each student on their current level of fitness. Even 40+ years later, I'm embarrassed to report I scored in the lowest passing grade for the test (bronze). If I had talent in any of the areas in which I would later focus, it wasn't obvious early on – to me or anyone else.

The notion that our destinies are, to a more or lesser extent, controlled by unseen factors, exerts a powerful influence on how we experience the world. It affects how we respond to challenges, the way we think about our goals and accomplishments, and how we interact with people.

This book is about talent - what it is, but maybe more importantly, what it's not. For at least the last 2400 years our thinking about talent has been focused on the contributions of innate biological factors – 'nature' – versus environmental and experiential factors – 'nurture'. Over the past two decades, my colleagues and I have studied this concept and its value for helping athletes and non-athletes achieve their goals in sport and life. We've examined how the amount and quality of practice affects the development of skill, as well as the role of parents, siblings, and coaches in helping maximize this practice. We've explored the role of an athlete's birthdate, whether they're right or left-handed, the size of the community they are born into, the length of their index finger compared to their ring finger (yes, that's a thing)[1] – all in an attempt to understand how and why some succeed while many others don't.

In addition to my scientific research, I've worked with high-performance teams and sport organizations to help them put this research into action. Often, this involves talent forecasting or working on athlete development programs aimed at providing teams and athletes with advantages over their competitors on the international stage. Much of this work is unpublished, but where I can, I'll provide general support for any conclusions I make using these practical applications.

Despite the range of research my colleagues and I have done in this area, this book wasn't easy to write. My job as a scientist is to evaluate evidence, write scientific papers, give lectures and teach students, but it's very rarely to conclude anything, especially about something like talent which has divided public and scientific opinion like few other topics. Scientific perspectives should always have an element of 'fence-sitting', not wanting to commit to a conclusion that might not bear the scrutiny of replication or the emergence of new data. There are obvious exceptions to this general rule (the 'theory' of evolution by natural selection is an example) but generally, we want researchers to be as open-minded as possible. That made the topic of this book – what can we *conclude* about talent and its role in understanding exceptional sporting accomplishments – difficult since I'm uncomfortable getting off the fence. Regardless, I'm going to try to convince you of a few things in the pages that follow. I'm going to try to convince you that talent is real. Despite what you might have read in many best-selling books published over the last two decades emphasizing the power of practice and experience, there are real differences between individuals that affect their likelihood of success, in sports and other domains.

I'm also going to try to convince you that the way we think about talent is wrong. Quite simply, the models we have for how talent operates across the processes of human and athlete development are not complex enough to explain these heavily nuanced progressions, which might explain why, even after thousands of years, we're still arguing about whether it's 'nature' or 'nurture' that is most important. These arguments have resulted in researchers and practitioners becoming entrenched in their thinking, a dangerous position regardless of whether you believe talent is generally fixed or highly flexible. This rigidity is what I refer to as the 'Tyranny of Talent'. Tyrannical approaches to, and beliefs about, athlete development are everywhere in sport. They are reflected in coaches' largely misguided searches for early signs of potential and dogmatic acceptance of 'the way it is' without challenging the evidence underpinning the dogma. They're also seen in the confidence many coaches have in their selections – often wrong, but never in doubt. We also see them reflected in the creation of simplistic 'one-size-fits-all' models that are used to govern systems for how athletes develop. At the heart of this tyranny is the over-simplification of one of the most complicated things coaches ever have to do – over-simplified by researchers or policymakers who are often far removed from the realities of how difficult a task this can be. The fields of talent science and athlete development are undergoing important shifts, but whether these shifts ultimately turn out to be good or bad will depend on what we learn from these circumstances.

Later in the book, I'll explore some options for improving the ways we structure and deliver sport, particularly at high performance levels. To help the reader understand these options, it's important to know how we got to the current state. I start by taking us back to the beginning of research in this area to describe the original conceptualizations of this topic, and how they set us on the wrong foot from the start. Later, I'll make the case for talent as an important variable for understanding differences in athletes' achievements, after which I'm going to try to convince you that we focus too much on it, and doing so, undermines the larger factors that ultimately end up having a greater impact on the performer and person we become.

The 'story' of talent is not finished, but at least now we know how to describe the characters. They're not the vague concepts of nature and nurture which have alternated in their roles of hero and villain in the story of human achievement. The influences of biology and experience are immensely complex and nuanced, requiring careful attention to understand how they influence our development and performance. There is potential here to not only understand how athletes are able to achieve feats of performance beyond most people's imagination, but also to understand a bit more about ourselves.

A note about anecdotes: In many popular science books anecdotes are used as if they were conclusive evidence to support a relationship/claim being promoted. Many scientists get frustrated with this type of discussion and spend a disproportionate amount of time explaining to the general public the limitations of applying one person's experience, and often a biased recollection of this experience, to all people (reflecting well known cognitive biases such as the 'availability heuristic' or the 'sharpshooter fallacy'). Herein, the recent or historically significant anecdotes that open many of the chapters are simply to anchor the discussion that follows.

"People are really surprised I understand this stuff," he said. "Every one of these doctors said, 'How do you know so much about this?' Maybe I have a natural ability."

Donald Trump on his handling of the COVID-19 crisis

Section I: The Set-Up

The well-known trope "those who don't know history are doomed to repeat it" applies well to the world of elite sport, where ideas continually emerge and re-emerge as generations of scientists change, and learnings are forgotten. Few active in the field today are aware of the scientific and philosophical foundations of talent, but these foundations are important. They explain how notions of talent have come to dominate discussions of human, and especially athlete, development the way they have. Although this section will focus on the historical highlights from psychology, education, and sport science, they generally reflect broader changes in how we try to understand and discuss elements of human nature. For over two millennia, philosophers have explored what makes humans the way they are, and it has only been relatively recently that we have seen a shift to a focus on why humans differ. Although both questions are critical for understanding human development and achievement, the focus by sport scientists on the latter without integrating relevant learnings regarding the former means our understanding will always be incomplete. And more critically, policies and programs for athlete development will be ill-conceived and ineffective.

In this section, Chapter 1 lays a broad foundation for discussing talent in sport before considering where this foundation comes from (in Chapters 2 and 3). The growth of research examining exceptional performance is the focus of Chapter 4, while Chapters 5 and 6 discuss the role of practice and genetic factors respectively.

Chapter 1. Needles and Haystacks

In 2011, the Internet was ablaze with the story of Baerke van der Meij, an 18-month-old 'soccer player' (if an 18-month-old can be 'called' anything other than a 'toddler') from the Netherlands who was signed to a 10-year symbolic contract with professional football club VVV Venlo. What made this story so fascinating was the youngster gained fame because of a YouTube video highlighting his remarkable skill at kicking plush balls into his toybox.[2] *It wasn't quite as ridiculous as it might seem. The boy's grandfather had a history with the same club suggesting a strong family connection. In an official statement the club stated "The toddler's favorite position has not yet been determined. But we can speak of a right-footed player with a very good kicking technique, perseverance and, importantly, football genes via his grandfather".*

...The search for talent starts early.

Talent, or the notion of being talented, means different things to different people and in different contexts. For researchers working in this area, this is an obvious problem. It's hard to measure something when we can't agree what it is we're trying to measure. That said, if we were to distill the essence of what 'talent' means for most people, we'd find it involves prediction, and these predictions involve time. At its most elemental, it's about seeing, measuring and evaluating something in the here and now and making a prediction about what it means for success in the future. This is done with surprising regularity – having elementary students take standardized tests to predict who is best suited for gifted education programs or having future elite athletes partake in a series of physical tests so recruiters, scouts and coaches can predict who is most likely to succeed at the professional level.

The notion of talent is writ large across the fabric of Western society. When we meet new people for the first time, we make predictions about them – am I going to enjoy talking to this person for more than a few seconds? (If no, I try to find a way to end the conversation quickly). When we have children, we watch their early learning behaviors and often make judgments about their future careers (look, she's chasing frogs. She's going to be a biologist, or naturalist, or veterinarian, or…). We have an entire genre of television that involves watching short segments of performance (singing in the case of shows like The Voice or American Idol) and predicting a performer's likelihood of long-term success.[3] Usually, these speculations are based on very limited exposure to the individual we're making the prediction about, but that usually doesn't stop us.

It's possible we're intrinsically wired to make these types of predictions. Rapid evaluation and judgement of different environmental stimuli likely served a critical survival role in our species' evolution. Early ancestors who didn't make quick enough decisions in a survival situation became some predator's lunch, not contributing much to the gene pool.

No domain of human endeavor embraces the concept of talent like sport. In most countries, the early identification and development of athletes with better potential for success ultimately limits how many athletes get the opportunity to chase their dreams of competing at the highest levels. In these models of talent development, youth are seen as commodities to be produced and refined while coaches are positioned as gatekeepers and designers of optimal training environments. These systems and early talent identification approaches are based on two assumptions. First, that talent is real and differs between individuals. The second assumption, which is far more relevant to those working in sports, education, music, and so on, is that we have good methods for measuring it. In the chapters that follow, we explore the evidence for, and implications of, both these assumptions.

Most people assume we know quite a lot about talent. It's central to how governments structure education (e.g., that those showing early proficiency are better bets for future success and should be streamed into 'gifted' programs), how employers think about employees (e.g., when they are seen as 'natural leaders' instead of assuming leadership is a skill to be developed) and, especially for our discussion, in the way we structure sport and athlete development systems. A few years ago, our research team undertook an extensive investigation of what we know about talent in sport. This process, called a systematic review, considered research conducted over a 25-year period. As it turns out, there is surprisingly little 'good' evidence testing this concept.[4] During the same period, interest in the concept of talent has increased considerably. The figure below shows the number of articles published on talent or talent-related outcomes in sport science journals.

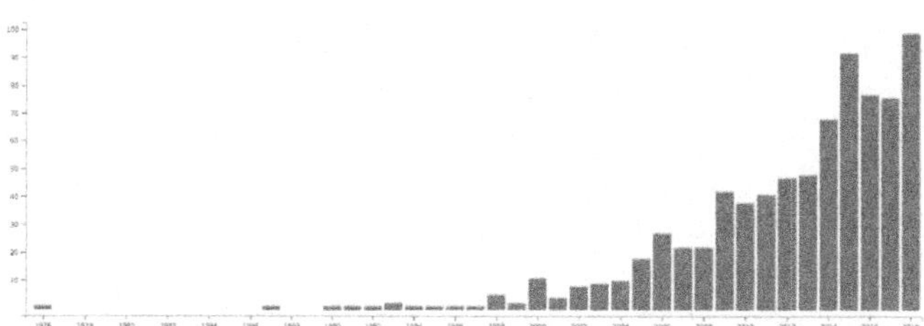

Number of articles with the keyword 'talent' published in peer-reviewed sport science journals between 1976 and 2018.[5]

What's immediately obvious is interest in talent is increasing. On the one hand, this is positive news because it reflects the curiosity scientists and sport stakeholders currently have for this concept. On the other, it emphasizes the lack of long-term attention to this issue – long-term attention that's necessary for researchers to have pushed and stretched this concept to build a strong evidence base for what's real and what's rhetoric. Science works best when teams of researchers compete, challenge, and argue with each other. Given the implications and consequences of how we think about talent in sport, a strong understanding of the gaps is vital. For instance, one of the most obvious questions athletes, or more likely their parents, should ask is "what is the likelihood of making it to the top?". Before mortgaging their homes to ensure their child-athlete has the best opportunities[6] parents should at least have some idea of how long the odds are.

In the table below, I've computed the odds of American athletes at different levels making it to the professional level in the four major professional sports in North America: the NBA, NHL, NFL and MLB. Without doubt, and perhaps unsurprisingly given the popularity of the sport and the number of available positions at the professional level, the NBA has the longest odds. The odds of a pre-high school player (often when talent identification and selection decisions start occurring) making it to the NBA are 1 in over 70,000. The NHL has the best odds; here a youth player has a 1 in just under 5,000 chance of making it to the pros.

Odds of Making It
Youth to Professional/Olympic Level

Professional Basketball	Youth 3,600,000	High School 541,479	College 18,697	Drafted 60	Play in NBA 51	**ODDS** 1 in 70588
Professional Football	Youth 4,700,000	High School 1,083,617	College 72,788	Drafted 254	Play in NFL 183	**ODDS** 1 in 25683
Professional Baseball	Youth 2,800,000	High School 486,567	College 34,198	Drafted 1,217	Play in MLB 329	**ODDS** 1 in 8511
Professional Ice Hockey	Youth 600,000	High School 35,875	College 4,071	Drafted 217	Play in NHL 124	**ODDS** 1 in 4839

Played in pros data comes from the % of drafted players who end up making it to the professional level of play. Estimates from Baker et al., 2012
Youth - data comes from 2019 National Sporting Goods Association participation data for the US.
High School and College - data come from Online Casino study
Drafted - comes from number of players drafted in 2019 draft
Note: youth football data include all levels of play (tackle, touch and flag). If we only include numbers from tackle football in youth, the odds are 1 in 6557
Note: the college, drafted and played in pros data are over-estimates for US players since these groups will also include players from other countries

In *No Hunger in Paradise*, journalist Michael Calvin's examination of youth football contexts in the UK, he estimates the odds of a developing youth in England making it to the premier league as just over 1 in 10,000.[7] Notably, a recent article found that 97% of players at elite football development academies do not play a single minute at the Premier League level.[8] All things considered, the odds of success are often much smaller than most anticipate.

The majority of parents, coaches and athletes do not have an 'all or nothing' mentality, where the professional level is seen as the only acceptable end point for athlete development; however, knowing these odds is still important. They provide stakeholders with estimates of success that should be considered relative to other issues. For instance, what sacrifices are we going to make to ensure the athlete is training in the 'best' environments for their continued development? Is 'professional athlete' a reasonable expectation that warrants these sacrifices compared to other career and life choices?

For most, these numbers are abstract without real-world examples to measure them against.[9] Consider the following – you are nearly two times more likely to win a prestigious Rhodes scholarship (1 in 37,500) than playing a minute in the NBA. Your odds of dying in the next 12 months due to a choking related accident (1 in 49,577) are also better than a pre-high school player has of ever making it to the NBA. To carry the absurdity even further, you have a greater chance of visiting the ER department in the next year due to a serious accident with a golf cart (1 in 22,325) or, if you are a working actor, a greater chance of winning an Academy Award (1 in 20,000) than a youth football player has of making the NFL. These comparisons are obviously silly, but that's the point. Athletes and their parents rarely consider how unlikely it is to make it from the youth to the professional level, yet they make incredible sacrifices all the same.

Undoubtedly, part of the reason they do this is because they believe they see indicators of talent at a young age. The key assumption these parents make (as do the coaches and scouts trying to identify early indicators of talent) is that these indicators are valid predictors of future success. This is on display when we see youth coaches tell parents their child has the gifts to 'go all the way' or when early development programs choose young top performers as better bets for long-term development. The problem is this relationship between early performance and long-term success is not supported by the available evidence, except in obvious examples. Consider sports where height is important for success. Peak adult height is a performance-related variable that is easily predicted in childhood using current height, indicators of maturity and standardized growth curves. On the one hand, being able to accurately predict a child's eventual height could be valuable in sports where adult stature is important (e.g., basketball, volleyball or rowing). However, height is not the only, or even the most important, variable for understanding elite performance in many of these sports. Most of the other factors necessary for future elite athletes cannot be reliably and validly predicted in youth.

The assumption that talent is obvious, that an athlete either has it or they don't, can be problematic for parents and coaches because they can make incorrect decisions about what they see, which can then affect how they interact with their athlete. These decisions end up having important implications for long-term development. Consider an athlete selected for the 'talented stream' in his local sports program (often called a 'representative team', or 'rep' for short). This simple outcome affects the quality of that athlete's training environment in subtle and not-so-subtle ways. The end results of these changes are referred to as "Matthew Effects" and are the focus of a later chapter, but let's consider the diverse ways these changes affect how that athlete sees himself. First, this messaging about being talented is likely reinforced by parents during conversations at home as well as with peers through the ways they interact with him at school or training. These messages enable a cascade of positive psychological changes including increased feelings of competence for his sport, amplified motivation and commitment to training and practice, and increased confidence during competition.[10] In addition to these psychological benefits, our athlete sees tangible improvements in the quality of his training environment. Now, he is training with the best athletes in the local area, travelling to compete with other representative teams - the breadth and depth of their exposure to competition has increased. In addition, 'rep' teams usually receive more practice time and better training facilities than teams at lower levels of competition. Over time, these differences add up, advantaging the player who is selected over the one who was not – despite the likelihood there were no real differences in 'potential' between them, or equally possible, the one who was deselected *had more talent but never got the chance to demonstrate this because of disadvantages imposed by the system*. We'll come back to these issues.

The most curious thing is that many coaches and parents appear to be aware of the flaws in the current athlete development system with its emphasis on early identification and selection. However, they regularly promote and encourage it through their continued participation and support of the current system. In this book, we will refer to this as the Standard Athlete Development (SAD) approach, which generally assumes some combination of the following: a) talent exists and needs to be identified so it can be nurtured, b) athletes progress through stages of development, with each stage delineated with regard to the most appropriate foci for learning and development, c) optimizing an athlete's development comes as the result of opportunities that are best delivered in structured and/or supervised environments, and d) the sooner we can get athletes into systematic programs of athlete development, the better it is for their development.

Several questions underpin most of the discussion throughout this text including 'does the existing evidence support the approaches most sports and sport systems use for athlete development?' and 'what are the consequences and implications of these approaches?'. In the next few chapters, we explore the early research in this area, which emerged from a general focus on the science of 'individual differences'. This early work had long-lasting impacts on how we think about athletes and their development.

Chapter 2. Untangling Talent

For to every one who has will more be given, and he will have abundance; but from him who has not, even what he has will be taken away
(Matthew 25:29 Revised Standard Version).

Modern conceptualizations of talent as a valued quality possessed by an individual likely comes from the 'parable of the talents' from the book of Matthew in the Bible's New Testament (believed to be written between 70 and 110 CE). The parable describes a landowner who goes on a trip and leaves his servants in charge of his money in the hopes that they will invest these funds wisely while he's away. When he returns, he evaluates how well each of the servants has managed his funds – did they increase as expected? Based on positive gains, two servants are rewarded. The third, who simply kept the goods safe while the landowner was away, is judged negatively. Over time, Christian teachings took this parable to mean each person is charged with the responsible 'investment' of the talents they are given, and may explain modern Christianity's focus on 'God given talents'.

Describing athletes as having 'natural talent' for sports like baseball or running is commonplace amongst fans, coaches, and athletes. A recent BBC article described Arsenal's signing of a 4-year-old to their football club's pre-academy, the youngest player ever to join their development system. The scout and coach in the article emphasized the young athlete's exceptional skill against others in his age group, and it was clear, compared to others at his level of development, he was exceptional. But is that 'talent'?[11] There is a surprising lack of clarity regarding what the word actually means, even among those whose jobs would seem to depend on a clear definition. One of the most amazing things we've learned in our research is the way this word is defined and conceptualized by coaches, athletes and parents is highly varied.

To be sure, there are similarities in how it's positioned, but the variation is quite telling.

In one of our earliest works in this area, we proposed talent as "the quality (or qualities) identified at an earlier point in time that promotes (or predicts) exceptionality at a future time".[12] However, while this definition likely reflects how most coaches, scouts and parents see talent, it's too vague to be very meaningful. For instance, it doesn't permit us to determine whether a current level of performance (i.e., where talent is being assumed) is the result of innate predispositions, learning experiences and training, or some combination of these factors.

This may seem trivial on the surface, but because sport scientists haven't done a very good job operationalizing this concept, a variety of possible definitions have filled this vacuum. In 2013, Ross Tucker of the popular *Science of Sport* website had visitors to their Facebook site respond to the question "What is talent?", generating a range of responses and a lack of clear descriptive characteristics.[13] Sport scientists haven't been much clearer. In addition to the vague definition we've used in the past that I mentioned above, others have defined it as "a special ability that allows someone to reach excellence in some activity in a given domain"[14] or even more generally as a "functional relationship developed between a performer and a specific performance environment".[15] While these various definitions reflect how talent is conceptualized by researchers and practitioners, particularly the latter one's focus on an individual's performance as a reflection of the interaction between performer, task and environment, the practical utility of these definitions for those working in high-performance sport environments is limited, if they have any value at all. More importantly, perhaps, the lack of an agreed upon definition makes it impossible to determine its value from the standpoint of scientific evidence. It's difficult to test the validity of something if we can't agree on what it is.

So, if we were to determine what talent means, where would we start? In some of our prior research, we asked coaches and trainers from varying levels of competition, working in different sports, with athletes from different ages and sexes, their views about talent to see where the commonalities lie. Most often, talent was restricted to physical attributes, perhaps not surprisingly since most research in sport science has focused on these types of measures. Others emphasized an athlete's 'coachability', although what that means isn't clear either.[16]

The lack of consensus on what talent 'is' and how it might be measured is not trivial. For scientists, the way we define and operationalize a concept is critical for designing appropriate studies and measures for evaluating it. As Carl Sagan notes in *The Demon Haunted World*, "If there's a chain of argument, every link in the chain must work (even the premise) – not just most of them".[17] Any faulty element in the 'chain of logic' undermines the entire argument. For researchers exploring the scientific basis for talent, there are limitations in how it has been conceptualized (i.e., from a philosophical perspective), how it has been operationalized (from a scientific perspective) and how it has been applied (from a practical perspective).

Talent as a philosophical concern

In its deepest form, the question of talent is an ontological one, ontology being the branch of philosophy that deals with whether things actually exist. This question, which seems so pertinent to much of how sport, education and society have been generally structured, is a recent one. That's not to say the notion of talent wasn't relevant in philosophical discussions – it was very relevant – but the way we think about what talent is and what it means has changed and taken on a much more substantive role in our lives. From an ontological perspective, the existence of talent requires there to be real differences between individuals, either in their innate state prior to any experience/learning or in how they learn/develop over time. From this perspective, talent could simply mean 'the thing that causes individuals to differ in meaningful ways' and this will be the perspective taken in this text (i.e., talent is real, people differ in it, and these differences are meaningful).

Acknowledging the commonalities and differences in how people use and define talent, and drawing connections to the historical and scientific record, it's impossible to have a fulsome discussion without first going through the longstanding debates about human nature. The notion of talent is inseparable from discussions about whether a person's behavior and accomplishments are the result of experiences and opportunities or predetermined at birth. Although this debate is generally framed as nature versus nurture, the historical nuances have been more complicated. The debate can be traced back at least as far as ancient Greece and arguments between Plato and Aristotle – Plato contending humans possess abstract knowledge and ideas that could not be reflected through simple sensory data and therefore such knowledge must be present at birth and Aristotle maintaining that sensory experiences were sufficient to explain the complex thoughts and reasoning people demonstrate.

Given our seemingly intrinsic drive to explain the world around us and our role in it, it's likely this debate continued in one form or another for the next 2000 years. Unsurprisingly, information on this topic throughout history is somewhat sparse until the arrival of the printing press in the mid-1400s. Prior to this time, debates about the roles of biology and environment were probably rare, given Christianity was the dominant Western worldview during this period. There is some discussion amongst such notables as St. Thomas Aquinas and St. Bonaventure, but it's not until the beginning of the enlightenment that we begin to see evidence of the strong re-emergence of this debate.

Rene Descartes (1596-1650), Baruch Spinoza (1632-1677), and Gottfried Wilhelm Leibnitz (1646-1716) were advocates of a view known as 'rationalism' which supported the view that certain aspects of cognition (i.e., reasoning) were innate. Around the same time period, Francis Bacon (1561-1626), John Locke (1632-1704), and David Hume (1711-1776) were developing a counter view of human nature grounded in the notion that human knowledge comes from experience. Locke famously proposed that humans begin as *tabula rasa* (Latin for 'scraped tablets'), and that knowledge and rules for navigating the world come purely from sensory experience. These enlightenment discussions highlight the on-going tug of war between social, political and scientific camps regarding whether our behavior, our potential, and ultimately our health and achievement are best explained by learning and experience or the mechanistic expression of our biology.

For the most part, these discussions were largely academic and philosophical, restricted to the thought leaders of the day. However, by the mid-1800s a convergence of factors profoundly influenced how this discourse would be shaped. Among other things, this convergence would have consequences for how we organize education and sport systems throughout the world. The basis for this convergence, and then extension, was the increasingly common use of the notion of talent as a key player in discussions of human nature.

Talent as a scientific concept

The word, *talent,* which is essentially synonymous with 'natural ability', has had an inconsistent history. The original usage of the word was as a major unit of weight; for example, a Greek talent was roughly equivalent to 56.9 pounds (25.8 kilograms). Over time, the meaning changed to refer to monetary value, simply as a measure of how much gold or silver something cost (e.g., the cost of X is a talent-weight of gold). At the time of this writing, gold costs $56.06 per gram and a Greek talent-weight of gold would cost approximately $1,613,532 USD.

Eventually, talent became akin to an aptitude or a capacity an individual possesses. This didn't happen quickly. According to the Oxford English Dictionary, the first use of the word 'talent' to refer to 'mental endowment or natural ability' [at least in English] was in the mid-15th century.[18] After this, there are sporadic uses in a range of English-language texts until the 1600s when talent becomes more widely used in a form like how it is used today.

It's not surprising to see the notion of talent as 'natural/innate ability' emerge during this time. Especially in the 19th century, there was a shift in how scientists and philosophers were considering questions of human nature due to advances in education and psychology. The emergence of talent as an explanation for differences between individuals led to a different type of discussion than had occurred previously. Instead of trying to understand humans as a group, the focus shifted to understanding humans as individuals. Predominantly, describing someone as having or not having talent relates to a field of science called 'individual differences' (i.e., the things that distinguish individuals from one another). You were unable to make the Olympics? Must be due to a lack of talent. Didn't achieve your goal of becoming a doctor (or artist or musician)? You must not have had the talent for it.

As we'll discuss in the next few chapters, developments in the philosophy of science, the precision of measurement, and the zeitgeist of the 19th and early 20th century lead to a magnified social need for variables that could explain why some succeeded when others did not, and to predict this success as a means of increasing social and industrial productivity.

Talent in practice

These broad social changes trickled down to all domains of education and instruction, especially sport. The rise of this perspective lead to talent becoming the 'thing selected for' in programs for talent development, gifted education, and employee recruitment. However, the role of 'selection' in physical tasks such as sport and military training is ancient. In ancient Sparta, the *agoge* was a means of identifying those who were more suited for key roles, largely military-related, in Spartan society. Even older, the Ancient Olympic Games allowed participants to compete against each other in a tribute to Zeus. Interestingly, the approach to the ancient Olympics and the agoge seemed to be relatively open (at least if you were male), unlike their contemporary counterparts, which emphasize exclusion. These ancient programs were used more broadly, open to all eligible male citizens. The underlying principle here seemed to be related to exposure – using the system to expose as many citizens as possible to training and education to see how they respond, and then using this response to determine their status as an athlete (as in the ancient Olympics) or in the society more generally (as in the agoge).

Unsurprisingly, the confusion, vagueness and inconsistency in what talent means for philosophers, scientists and practitioners results in athlete development environments that are confusing, vague and inconsistent. These are not new problems. However, the difficulties with talent may be traced to the scientific foundations of this field of research, which set the standards for discourse and empirical study of this phenomenon. We'll get into these specific measurement issues and limitations about talent in due course, but it's important to establish that the ways in which scientists conceptualize and set out to measure a variable can determine whether they find what they are looking for.

In 1939, renowned astrophysicist Arthur Eddington proposed the following parable about a scientist of ichthyology:

> Let us suppose that an ichthyologist is exploring the life of the ocean. He casts a net into the water and brings up a fishy assortment. Surveying his catch, he proceeds in the usual manner of a scientist to systematise what it reveals. He arrives at two generalisations: (1) No sea-creature is less than two inches long. (2) All sea-creatures have gills. These are both true of his catch, and he assumes tentatively that they will remain true however often he repeats it.
>
> In applying this analogy, the catch stands for the body of knowledge which constitutes physical science, and the net for the sensory and intellectual equipment which we use in obtaining it. The casting of the net corresponds to observation; for knowledge which has not been or could not be obtained by observation is not admitted into physical science.
>
> An onlooker may object that the first generalisation is wrong. "There are plenty of sea-creatures under two inches long, only your net is not adapted to catch them." The icthyologist dismisses this objection contemptuously. "Anything uncatchable by my net is ipso facto outside the scope of icthyological knowledge. In short, what my net can't catch isn't fish."

Eddington's analogy highlights the limits of setting standards of measurement and then having to stick to those standards. Scientists (mostly) and coaches (partly) are at fault for creating a system for defining the reality of what talent is. This creates problems at a fundamental level for understanding this concept. Consider the following chain of events: You believe talent relates to physical elements of performance and generate a series of tests to assess these elements (e.g., sprint and power assessments, tests of endurance, etc.). Scores on these tests are then used to select athletes to move on in your system (i.e., those with higher scores move on, those with lower scores are removed). To test the accuracy and validity of your assessments, you look at who was most successful at the elite level and determine your tests were valid predictors of talent since those with the highest physical scores made it to the elite level.

Not so fast! The way talent was conceptualized in the beginning (as physical) affected how its validity was determined. Focusing on the physical (our 'net', to use Eddington's example) limits the way we approach measuring the variables of interest. As you'll see in the next few chapters, the definitions of what talent is, or might be, have changed considerably since it was first conceptualized in the 19th century and the way we've framed talent is important for determining the evidence for and against this concept.

You could be forgiven for being pessimistic about the situation in youth sport, with its focus on early athlete identification and selection, which many have referred to as a 'race to the bottom'. However, while the notion of what talent is, and how it affects our development and attainment, is a deep problem, improving youth sport may not be. However, before we get there, we need to understand the roots of the issue.

Chapter 3. Blame Galton

In 2011, two psychologists from Harvard University, Chia-Jung Tsay and Mahzarin Banaji, designed a series of experiments to "understand what experts pay attention to when making decisions about talent and achievement and whether their stated beliefs and preferences are consistent with their actual choices"[19]. They were interested in individuals' beliefs about two well-known sources of achievement – natural talent and hard work (which they called 'striving') – and whether peoples' beliefs were reflected in ratings they made about the quality of individual performers. In one of their experiments, one hundred and three elite musicians were presented with a profile and 20 second sample of piano playing from two musicians and were asked to rate each musician on four items – perceived talent, likelihood of success, response to adversity, and willingness to hire the musician. Unbeknownst to the participants, the piano samples were taken from the same person and the profiles were constructed to reflect beliefs about talent, that is they emphasized either a performer with natural gifts or someone who achieved their skill through hard work.

Their results showed that, unsurprisingly, we value hard work. The musicians rated hard work as being more important than having natural talent. However, when it came time to evaluate the musical pieces, they over-valued the performance of the 'natural' – despite the fact that both pieces were by the same individual. We may say we value the 'striver' but when it comes to making a decision about who is more talented and likely to succeed, we're biased towards the natural.

From a scientific standpoint, the way we think about and conceptualize talent largely remain stuck in paradigms from over 150 years ago. In 1865, Macmillans Magazine published a two-part article entitled "*Hereditary Character and Talent*" by a gentleman scientist named Francis Galton. Although he was little known at the time (outside a few niche geographic and/or scientific circles, at least), history would eventually view the future Sir Francis as many things; *polymath*, *father of modern statistics*, and *genius* are certainly suitable descriptors, equally so may be *bigot*, *racist*, and *monster*. At this point in history, however, he was largely known for writing detailed travel essays and identifying strange geographical phenomena. The article in Macmillans represented a major turning point in Galton's life and would go on to establish him as a leader in multiple domains of science, including talent, genetics, twin and family studies, as well as applied statistics, historiometry and psychometrics.

Galton was born in south-east Birmingham, England on February 16, 1822 to a family well-known for its contributions to scientific discourse. He was the paternal grandson of Samuel Galton Jr., a Quaker and arms manufacturer, and maternal grandson of Erasmus Darwin, a well-known physician, botanist, inventor and poet. Both his grandfathers were members of the Lunar Society, one of the earliest scientific organizations in England (formed in 1765) that met only during full moons.[20] Erasmus Darwin was a founding member of the society and one of earliest proponents of a more scientific worldview emphasizing species evolution over extended periods of time. With other members, which included such notables as Josiah Wedgwood (founder of Wedgwood pottery), Joseph Priestley (theologian and philosopher perhaps best known as co-discoverer of oxygen), William Withering (physician and inventor of digitalis), and James Watt (inventor and engineer, known best for developing the concept of horsepower and the unit of power known as the watt), Erasmus Darwin was a key figure in the movement linking the scientific revolution of the 18th century with the industrial revolution, ending in the mid-19th century.

It's not surprising Galton eventually ended up focusing on the field of talent and exceptional achievement; he had all the signs of being a prodigy himself. Reports have him reading by the age of two, knowing elements of Latin and Greek by the age of 5 and reading Shakespeare for pleasure by the age of 6. A retrospective estimate suggests his childhood IQ was 200[21], considerably higher than similar estimates of scientific notables such as Charles Darwin (165), Copernicus (160) and Galileo (185)[22]. Without doubt, Galton was raised in an environment of exceptional privilege and wealth, which allowed young Francis the independence to explore a diverse range of interests. By his mid-twenties, he was financially independent and established as one of the leading geographers and explorers in England. His book *The Art of Travel*, published in 1855, provided an extensive handbook of practical travel advice (e.g., how to cross a river with a horse[23]) that went through five editions and remains in print today. During this period - the 'geographer and explorer' phase of Galton's life - he also made major contributions to meteorology and weather, including the creation of the world's first weather map in 1861, which has been a mainstay of newspaper weather sections ever since. In examining the impressive host of prominent Victoria scientists during the period, it's hard to find someone with a more diverse and notable resume of accomplishments than Galton.

Another factor that makes the article in Macmillans so noteworthy is the topic. This is the first known scientific investigation into the field of talent. Its premise, that "talent is transmitted by inheritance in a very remarkable degree" was radical at the time, although the world was ripe for this type of article. Charles Darwin (Galton's half-cousin) had recently published (in 1859) *On the Origin of Species*, a work that forever changed how we view and explain the world. It also profoundly altered the course of Galton's life. In a letter to Darwin just after the book was published, Galton writes "Pray let me add a word of congratulation on the completion of your wonderful volume… I have laid it down in the full enjoyment of a feeling that one rarely experiences after boyish days…". For Darwin, the mechanism of species' evolution was *natural selection*, reflecting the likelihood that members of a species that were better suited to their developmental environment were more likely to survive and reproduce. The power of Darwin's theory can be found in its simplicity and breadth; everything from explaining differences in beak length within the same bird species (finches were Darwin's favourite[24]) to understanding why the colour red may lead to more success in sporting contests[25] can be explained via this theory. Evolution has become so crucial for understanding the biological world that Theodosius Dobzhansky, one of the most accomplished evolutionary biologists of the 20th century concluded "Nothing in biology makes sense except in the light of evolution".[26]

For Galton though, it was Darwin's first chapter on 'Variation under Domestication' that captured his attention. The chapter explored the ways humans have constrained, through luck as well as science, the development of different animal species. We see Darwin's impact early in the article.

Galton begins:

> The power of man over animal life, in producing whatever varieties of form he pleases, is enormously great. It would seem as though the physical structure of future generations was almost as plastic as clay, under the control of the breeder's will. It is my desire to show, more pointedly than – so far as I am aware – has been attempted before, that mental qualities are equally under control.

He goes on to conclude human qualities of character were open to the same level of control as aspects of animal behavior were to selective breeding programs. Galton's argument begins by comparing the obvious physical similarities between parents and offspring before making something of a leap in logic in assuming that the same similarities would be found in non-physical qualities.

This era of scientific achievement was driven by the need to establish clear laws governing the measurable world and Galton was surely motivated by the need for the type of elegant and precise explanation of inheritance as his cousin had found for explaining variation in the natural world. To his mind, the obvious heritability of physical qualities such as stature pointed to principles that would explain variation in other less obvious qualities (e.g., his vague notion of 'character'). They simply required appropriate vigor and attention, as well as uncovering suitable statistical and methodological tools.

> Everyone who has trained himself to physical exercises discovers the extent of his muscular powers to a nicety. When he begins to walk, to row, to use the dumb bells, or to run, he finds to his great delight that his thews strengthen, and his endurance of fatigue increases day after day. As long as he is a novice, he perhaps flatters himself there is hardly an assignable limit to the education of his muscles; but the daily gain is soon discovered to diminish, and at last it vanishes altogether...There is a definite limit to the muscular powers of every man, which he cannot by any education or exertion overpass.[27]

Galton began his exploration by identifying lists of notable individuals from well-known reference biographies of the time and evaluating these lists to determine the extent to which exceptionality (i.e., being selected for entry in a notable biography) clustered within family members. His initial search focused on general lists of notable Englishmen, observing that the likelihood of having a relative also on the list was between 1 in 7 and 1 in 3.5.[28] We could quickly do a similar examination of the relationship between parents and their children in sport – for example, Delino DeShields and Delino DeShields Jr., Ken Griffey Sr. and Ken Griffey Jr., Mark Leiter and Mark Leiter Jr., and Cal Ripken Sr. and Cal Ripken Jr. – if we just limit our list to fathers and sons who played Major League Baseball and *have the same name*. A recent study from our research team found that parents of elite athletes were more likely to have been elite athletes themselves.[29] While these results support a relationship between parents and their offspring, they don't necessarily prove the importance of good familial genes.

An obvious limitation to this type of analysis is that you cannot separate the effects of a beneficial genetic profile (i.e., the biological contribution from great parents) from the environmental effects that come from exceptional achievement (e.g., higher standards of living which may result in more opportunities). Interestingly, in sport settings, elite offspring often excel in sports that are different than those in which their parents excelled; NFL Quarterback Randall Cunningham's son and daughter are elite high jumpers, Pole-vaulter Sergey Bubka's son (Sergei) is a professional tennis player, and ice-hockey player Ted Irvine's son is professional wrestler Chris Jericho.

Galton wasn't ignorant of the possibility of the environment confounding his argument, but he was quick to dismiss these influences. By comparing domains that he thought were high in nepotism (such as politics) with those that were not (such as literature and science), he concluded that the greater likelihood of being from an exceptional family across these diverse domains reflected genetic advantages, not environmental ones. Galton assumed that because children of eminent persons were more likely to become eminent themselves this reflected a heritable mechanism. For achievement in science and literature, for example, he notes "there is no favour here beyond the advantage of a good education". Interestingly, Galton created the earliest forms of correlation analysis to show the strength of relationships between these types of variables and, unfortunately, becomes the very first victim of the classic undergraduate error of confusing correlation with causation. In this case, he assumes that because two variables are related, and one occurs temporally before the other, that the first must have caused the second. He hasn't ruled out any of the potential other reasons for the relationship between these variables and therefore runs the risk of what is known as a 'third cause fallacy' (i.e., that the reason for the association is due to another variable, such as beneficial environments). Undoubtedly, family effects are diverse and multi-faceted, ranging from providing a home environment with a clear value structure (e.g., involvement in certain activities over others) and support for education and training, to hereditary effects on variables ranging from intelligence and work ethic to exercise capacity and the proportion of different types of muscle fibers. It is also likely these variables cannot be easily separated into genetic versus environmental factors since opportunity and biology interact to create an individual's developmental environment (more on this later).

Galton's intellectual life and work changed direction completely after this article. His persistent fascination with talent, genius and heredity also fueled a desire for social improvement through purposefully selecting the most talented (i.e., those with the greatest potential for improving society) as mates. This movement to controlled, social breeding – hardly radical in a Victorian England that viewed itself with a certain degree of intellectual superiority over the rest of the world – would underpin several of the worst atrocities of the 20th century. Programs that forced sterilization of the simple or feeble minded, for example, were widespread in countries like the United States and Canada and the 'eugenics movement' (i.e., advocating the improvement of the human species via selectively mating people with desirable, heritable traits) provided a biological and ideological philosophy for the Nazi 'final solution' of World War II.[30]

This potential for controlling the evolutionary process was the element of Darwin's text that captured Galton's monumental energies and focus. His later books would expand on the notion of eugenics but the seeds of this were planted early. In the Macmillan's article, he imagines a world of the future where the 10 brightest young men in the nation assemble before a government representative who passionately states:

> Gentlemen, I have to announce the results of a public examination, conducted on established principles; which show that you occupy the foremost places in your year, in respect to those qualities of talent, character, and bodily vigour which are proved, on the whole, to do most honour and best service to our race. An examination has also been conducted on established principles among all the young ladies of this country who are now of the age of twenty-one, and I need hardly remind you, that this examination takes note of grace, beauty, health, good temper, accomplished housewifery, and disengaged affections, in addition to noble qualities of heart and brain. By a careful investigation of the marks you have severally obtained, and a comparison of them, always on established principles, with those obtained by the most distinguished among the young ladies, we have been enabled to select ten of their names with especial reference to your individual qualities. It appears that marriages between you and these ten ladies, according to the list I hold in my hand, would offer the probability of unusual happiness to yourselves, and, what is of paramount interest to the State, would probably result in an extraordinarily talented issue. Under these circumstances, if any or all of these marriages should be agreed upon, the Sovereign herself will give away the brides, at a high and solemn festival, six months hence, in Westminster Abbey. We, on our part, are prepared, in each case, to assign 5000£ as a wedding-present[31], and to defray the cost of maintaining and educating your children, out of the ample funds entrusted to our disposal by the State.

While this initiative doesn't do much for notions of Victorian romance, Galton's focus was on social improvement and how the advancing knowledge of evolution could be used to improve the lot of his own species. That said, his arguments don't work without first making the case for talent.

Galton's musings in this area (contained in this article and expanded upon in his best-known book *Hereditary Genius*) have been amazingly enduring. For example, consider the basic presumption of his work which positions talent as a reflection of a person's potential for a given activity or domain (e.g., a talent for music). This notion is grounded in assumptions that talent is fixed and easily measured, generally the way most people think about this concept. Unfortunately, as we'll see in more detail in later chapters, neither of these assumptions is accurate. An individual's talent for a domain is something that emerges and evolves across development and is nearly impossible to identify early, except in domains where performance is determined by relatively simple variables.

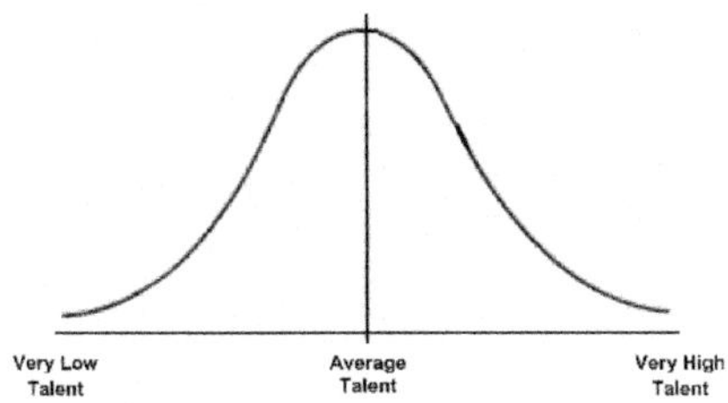

The normal distribution

Galton was also among the first to ground his approach in the Gaussian distribution, which later became commonly known as the 'normal distribution' or the 'bell curve'. This distribution (reflected in the figure above) indicates the majority of scores in a population will occur around the mean (or average) with a decreasing proportion of scores as you move toward each end of the distribution. When talent is positioned as representing individuals at the far-right hand side of the normal distribution, it is also positioned as rare compared to the majority of the population.

Perhaps the most durable supposition about talent is that qualities affecting an individual's potential for achievement can be easily separated into factors transmitted via hereditary mechanisms (these would eventually be termed 'genetic factors' although genes were not identified during Galton's lifetime) and factors that relate to the quality of one's environment. Even Galton uses this dichotomy of nature versus nurture in the title of one of his subsequent books (*English Men of Science: Their Nature and their Nurture*). This division has been the dominant framework for exploring factors influencing human achievement.

This dominance may not have been entirely Galton's doing. Although his initial research became a flashpoint for work in this area, after the 1869 publication of *Hereditary Genius*, the rate of research progressed so quickly that Galton eventually gave up trying to update later editions of the book.[32] There's also evidence that Galton's own views on the supremacy of nature over nurture mellowed over time. Regardless, the notion persists that explanations and methodological approaches to measurement can be cleanly divided into factors related to the environment and those related to innate qualities. In addition to their widespread use in most areas of science, these simple dichotomies have become popular ways of framing issues in athlete development where complex problems are framed in overly simplistic ways (e.g., nature vs nurture, play vs practice, specialization vs sampling). Richard Dawkins refers to this as the Tyranny of the Discontinuous Mind, reflecting our brain's propensity to cleanly divide the world into binary categories (wrong vs right, democrat vs republication, and, yes, talented or untalented).[33] Fortunately, these simplistic positions are becoming increasingly criticized as being poor representations of the complexity they are meant to reflect. Like a regrettable tattoo, however, the mark of Galton's influence has been difficult to remove.

Chapter 4. Scientific Ivory Hunters

Galton's research was just the first step along a path that has limited how we view talent and its development. In addition to Galton's initial contributions to this new science of talent, the timing of the publication of Darwin's Origin of Species, and the social movement toward racial de-segregation following the American abolition of slavery during the American Civil War, did much to set the course this field of study would follow for the next 100 years. This period of history was a time of massive social change in Western societies. The fact that these social movements occurred immediately before World War I set the stage for an unprecedented focus on assessing and evaluating men in the most efficient way possible.

In 1917, as the United States prepared to enter World War I, representatives of the American Psychological Association and the National Research Council's Committee for Psychology developed approaches to measure soldiers' innate potential for the myriad jobs required by this new, more global form of warfare. Unlike in previous conflicts where physical capabilities were critical, this new field of battle would require men capable of making smart and rapid decisions. As noted "speed counts in a war that costs 50 million dollars per day".[34] *To this end, the objectives of this initiative were to design easy-to-administer tests: "(a) to aid in segregating the mentally incompetent, (b) to classify men according to their mental capacity, (c) to assist in selecting competent men for responsible positions".*[35] *Ultimately, this would result in the creation of tests to measure the intelligence of prospective soldiers so they could be quickly and accurately placed into appropriate roles. Two tests were devised; the first, the Army Alpha measured a recruit's verbal and numerical abilities as well as their ability to follow directions, and knowledge of information. Recruits who were not able to understand the Army Alpha (e.g., those who were illiterate or did not speak English, which made up about 30% of recruits) undertook the Army Beta, a nonverbal equivalent of the Alpha test. In all, over 1.7 million recruits took either the Alpha or the Beta test. The age of mass standardized testing had arrived.*

The culmination of a diverse range of social factors at the dawn of the 20th century stimulated a focus on stable, innate factors to explain differences in human achievement. The early 1900s saw the first scales to measure intelligence, a general mental capacity described as "the ability to reason, plan, solve problems, think abstractly, comprehend complex ideas, learn quickly and learn from experience".[36] Like Galton's notion of hereditary ability or talent, intelligence was positioned as a fixed capacity that could be used to predict an individual's potential for success. The first tool to measure intelligence in a valid, reliable, and standardized way was created by Alfred Binet in 1905. Binet was a French psychologist focused on evaluating children with learning disabilities. France had recently passed a law requiring school attendance for all children under the age of 15, and, as a result, educators needed to have a way of determining the correct level of education for students' abilities. The Binet-Simon test (Theodore Simon was a medical student and research assistant of Binet's who helped him create the original test) filled this need and established many of the tenets still used for measuring intelligence today, such as performing tasks of increasing difficulty to determine the limits of a person's capacity and comparing a person's score to normative data reflecting their peer group.

Due to its ease of use and ability to standardize individual scores using population norms, the Binet-Simon test was rapidly taken up by educators and researchers in the United States. As noted earlier, the onset of World War 1, amongst other cultural and social changes occurring during this time, lead to an increased focus on ways large numbers of people could be evaluated for things like suitable employment, education, and healthcare.[37] Binet's view of intelligence, however, was different from how the concept was operationalized by WW1 psychologists, and how it is considered today. Binet's research focused on case studies and so he saw intelligence as extraordinarily complex and highly variable across contexts. Although the test would later become famous as a population-related measure of intellectual potential, Binet appears to have had little interest in developing a generalizable tool with application beyond his focus on learning disabilities.

The change from examining intelligence as a general approach for understanding the unique needs of an individual to its current conceptualization as a general proxy of one's intellectual potential is, in no small part, due to the work of Charles Spearman and Lewis Terman. Spearman, an English psychologist and statistician, began his career as a soldier, retiring at the age of 34 to commence a PhD under Wilhelm Wundt at the University of Leipzig. Spearman's dissertation first formulated the hypothesis that the various measures of cognition being used at this time might collectively reflect a single capacity, which he called 'g' for *general intelligence factor.* To test this hypothesis, he created a statistical technique called a 'factor analysis' that is widely used to test the stability of psychological tests.

Essentially, a factor analysis looks for patterns of relationships between variables in a larger dataset. Consider, for example, a dataset that includes results of grade 5 students on a battery of physical and cognitive tests showing a common element that related to how students scored on different measures. It might show that performance on tests of cognitive functioning or endurance performance were related, with students scoring similarly across these tests. This suggests a common 'factor' that underlies or influences students' cognitive functioning and endurance performance.[38]

Spearman was investigating a pattern he noticed in data from children's scores on a range of different tests, specifically that tests scores were positively correlated even for tests that were unrelated. Spearman created his factor analysis approach to test the validity of his observation that there seemed to be a common variable underlying performance on cognitive tasks. His analysis led to a simple two factor model; the first factor contained a general aspect (simply called 'g') that would capture the part of intelligence that overlapped across the tests, and a second aspect reflecting variables that were specific to performance on this test. The 'g factor' became increasingly popular for understanding human potential as it suggested a common element that underpinned performance on a range of endeavours.[39]

Armed now with this general approach to measuring intellectual potential, a generation of psychologists began exploring the application of this work. The most influential of which was, arguably, Lewis Terman, one of the American psychologists responsible for creating and implementing the Army Alpha and Beta tests. Terman was a colossal figure in American Psychology in the first half of the 20th century. His famous *Genetic Studies of Genius*, begun in 1921, tracked a sample of over 1500 youth identified with high IQ using a modification of the original scale designed by Binet. This study sought to understand how early indicators of intelligence related to indicators of development and success. The longest continuous examination in history, the study has continued to track this original sample (informally known as the "Termites") as they've moved through the various stages of life.

All this to say, at this time the science of human skill acquisition was heavily focused on the role of innate qualities in underpinning achievement. Achievement in physical domains was no different. Like those created to measure an individual's intellectual capacity, tests were created to determine an individual's capacity to perform movement tasks. In 1927, for example, David Kingsley Brace published the influential "*Measuring Motor Ability*" which outlined a series of tests to capture one's ability to perform motor/movement tasks. From the onset,

Brace positioned his concept of motor ability as the physical equivalent of intelligence, "corresponding on the physical side to mental ability, on the intelligence side of human activity".[40] The motor ability tests were designed to "assist physical educators in the classification of their pupils, in furnishing a basis upon which to evaluate achievement, and in gaining a better understanding of the motor side of human reactions" and as such reflected the dominant position of the time - that performance in physical tasks (including sport) was underpinned by stable and measurable physical capacities akin to how intelligence was being positioned in cognitive domains. It's important to highlight the difference between Brace's concept of a motor *ability* and a motor *skill*. Researchers in this area see motor abilities as relating to more general traits or capacities (e.g., simple reaction time) that contribute to performance on a range of outcomes, while motor skills relate to the specific skill being performed (anticipating an opponent's forthcoming action in tennis or wrestling by 'reading' their body position).[41] Importantly, motor abilities are not normally influenced (at least to any large extent) by training, while motor skills are.

The notion that a single global ability would underlie performance in all physical tasks has been enduring. It's the assumption we make when we call people 'natural athletes', as if performance in all sports originates from a common cause. It also certainly underlies traditional viewpoints on sporting talent. The original conceptualization of talent only makes sense when discussed as a general capacity; the idea that someone might have a talent for a single domain (e.g., a talent for basketball) that doesn't affect performance in other areas doesn't fit with our understanding of how evolution works. Evolution by natural selection is a thrifty process and it makes more sense that any evolutionary adaptations that would affect sporting performance would cross sport boundaries (i.e., showing up in multiple sports that share similar characteristics).

Furthermore, there is clear evidence that genetic factors can impede performance. Developmental Coordination Disorder, for example, is a neurological disorder that affects planning and execution of motor actions. It affects about 5% of school-aged children but continues to impair motor system function across the lifespan. Well-known sufferers include actors Daniel Radcliffe and Cara Delevinge and research suggests a clear genetic component to the disorder.[42] Logically, if there is high heritability (i.e., variation in a trait in a population is largely explained by genetic factors, a concept we return to later) for factors that impede function at a general level, it would follow that a similar relationship would affect exceptional capabilities. Surprisingly then, there isn't great support for the concept of a general motor ability. Correlational studies examining the relationships between performance in even closely related skills show very little overlap. One well known study in this area found no relationship between different tests of balance, even when the tests were very similar, such as walking on a balance beam from a forward versus sideward approach.[43] Moreover, the confirmatory evidence that does exist suggests the value of this general underlying ability decreases with age, meaning it's more important in explaining differences between individuals early in life, becoming less important with age.[44]

At around the same time, at the University of Iowa, a contemporary of Brace's, Charles McCloy, was exploring a different approach. Contrary to Brace, who felt that the ability to perform motor tasks was largely innate, McCloy felt individuals differed in their *ability to learn* how to perform motor tasks, a concept he called 'motor educability'. This he defined as "the ability to learn motor skills easily and well. It corresponds, in the area of general-motor skills, to intelligence in the area of classroom subjects". In a widely used early textbook on measurement in health and physical education, McCloy and Young described motor educability as consisting of 25 elements, ranging from motor and sensory rhythm, arm control and accuracy of direction as well as timing and quick decision-making. In addition to these elements, they noted 11 'prerequisites' for successful learning including broad components such as muscular strength and ability, as well as more specific psychological and cognitive factors like the 'ability to perceive objects with reasonable clarity out in the edge of the visual field', 'ability to concentrate or to keep the mind on an activity' and the 'absence of disturbing or inhibiting emotional complications such as fear of the water in learning to swim'.[46]

On the face of it, if we were able to determine who had the greatest ability to learn or adapt to training, this would be an important predictor of ultimate attainment. However, like the notion of a general motor ability, this approach was unsuccessful in identifying a capacity that would explain why some succeed and others do not. That said, at its most basic, this concept still views potential as easily quantifiable and predictable from performance on a test (or series of tests) measured at one point in time, giving only superficial acknowledgement of the complicated architecture of physiology, cognition, and psychology that underpins long-term learning.

The work in the period from 1905 when Binet developed the first intelligence test, to the 1950s when physical education researchers were mired in explorations of general capacities of motor ability and motor educability, reflected the strong focus of the time on innate, biologically-driven explanations for human performance. However, things were about to change.

> The secret of Babe Ruth's ability to hit is clearly revealed in these tests. His eye, his ear, his brain, his nerves all function more rapidly than do those of the average person. Further the coordination between eye, ear, brain, and muscle is much nearer perfection than that of the normal healthy man. The scientific 'ivory hunters' dissecting the 'home run king'

> discovered brain instead of bone, and showed how little mere luck, or even mere hitting strength, has to do with Ruth's phenomenal record.
> *Hugh S. Fullerton writing in Popular Science magazine in 1921*[47]

Babe Ruth was the greatest slugger in the history of baseball and arguably the finest baseball player of all time. While we often romanticize the past despite evidence that performance in most sports continues to evolve to higher levels of ability, Ruth reigns supreme as baseball's "sultan of swat". For over 30 years (1927-1961), Babe held the record for 'most official home runs during the regular season' (60), a record that has only been eclipsed by 4 players in history, Roger Maris (in 1961), Sammy Sosa (in 1998 and 1999), Mark McGuire (in 1998 and 1999) and Barry Bonds (in 2001).[48] Ruth's other achievements are simply extraordinary – hitting 40+ home runs in 11 seasons, 714 career home runs (only Barry Bonds and Hank Aaron have hit more home runs in their careers), 7 division pennants and four world series titles. No one has ever hit home runs as far and as consistently as 'the Babe' – not even close. Over the entire history of baseball, no one has hit more homers over 450 feet; amazingly, there is strong evidence that on October 12, 1926 Babe Ruth hit a home run that traveled over 600 feet, possibly 650 feet. This is about 20-25% longer than the longest home runs ever hit by the likes of Sammy Sosa, Mark McGuire or Barry Bonds. Put simply, Babe Ruth was a home run machine.

Charles Herman 'Babe' Ruth was born on February 6, 1895 in Baltimore, Maryland into a family with strong German roots. Little is known about Ruth's childhood apart from vague and usually trivial details such as his father's employment (a range of short-term jobs, including lightning rod salesman and streetcar operator before opening a saloon), Babe's trouble with authority (he was sent to reform school at the age of 7), and his early vocational training as a carpenter and shirt-maker. It was during his time at St. Mary's Industrial School for Boys that Ruth met

Brother Matthias Boutlier, Prefect of Discipline at the school. Boutlier, originally from Nova Scotia, Canada, was the person responsible for introducing Babe to sports, particularly baseball. On several occasions Babe would note Boutlier as his role model for his unique hitting and running styles. Ruth would estimate that he played 200 games a year as a student at St. Mary's, playing a range of positions before ultimately emerging as a pitcher. Although he did not seem to have received any specific training as a pitcher, he excelled in this position. He signed his first professional contract as a pitcher with the Baltimore Orioles, at the time a minor league triple A team.

To many historians, the most impressive season of Babe's career was in 1921. In his excellent book on Ruth, Bill Jenkinson suggests that if Babe Ruth had played his 1921 season under modern baseball rules and in a modern ballpark, he would have hit 104 home runs. It was also during this year that Babe and legendary sportswriter Hugh Fullerton spent an evening at the Columbia University Psychological Laboratory where Ruth underwent a series of tests to figure out the secret to his phenomenal batting skill.

This event was remarkable not only for the fact that it involved a scientific analysis of the most famous athlete in the world at the time, although this alone makes it one of the most notable 'case studies' in the history of sport science. It also involved a very significant laboratory in the history of psychology in the United States. It was established by the United States' first professor of psychology, James Cattell, in 1891. Cattell's work focused on the emerging science of 'differential psychology' – a field of psychology that focuses on understanding the ways individuals differ psychologically. Although Cattell was no longer at Columbia in 1921 (he was fired in 1917 for his opposition to America's conscription policy during World War I), the lab maintained its focus in this area. During Babe's visit, the lab was run by Robert S. Woodworth, who trained under Cattell and was an early pioneer of the science of measurement (known as 'psychometrics') and how learning in one context might transfer to others.[49]

Perhaps most importantly, this study represents the first psychological study of a professional athlete with the purpose of understanding their exceptional talent. As with much research at the time, there was a clear focus on measuring general capacities thought to underpin one's motor ability. For instance, one of the tests measured Babe's hand-eye coordination and movement accuracy using a triangular board with a series of small randomly placed holes. The task involved moving successively from one hole to the next jabbing a handheld mental probe into each hole as quickly as possible for one minute. According to the lab's normative data for non-athletes (82 holes touched in one minute), Babe Ruth's scores (122 for his right hand and 132 with his left) demonstrated his superior "hand, brain, and eye".

These tests represented where thinking was focused during this period of psychology – specifically that differences in the performance of individuals on general tasks such as those that measure simple reaction time, movement time, and response time, would reflect stable differences in the rates of information processing and/or movement execution that could explain differences in sport performance. Similar tests were done around the same time and in the same lab with legendary golfer Walter Hagen and boxer Harry Wills. Interest in these types of tests as reflecting factors that might explain exceptional performance continues; baseball superstar Albert Pujols underwent the "Babe Ruth Test" in 2006, revealing his superiority in several areas including a finger tapping measure of gross motor performance and a letter cancellation task that measures one's ability to search a visual display for a target letter.

What these tasks have to do with baseball performance is unclear and their overall value for understanding the skills and capabilities of elite baseball players is highly suspect. Over the past half century, research has been remarkably consistent, highlighting the lack of difference between performers at different levels of skill on many of these general measures. Simple reaction time, for example, does not generally differ between samples of individuals, no matter how skilled or unskilled the groups are. This is very important and bears emphasizing given the common belief in the general public that top athletes must have some impressive capacity to react in the blink of an eye – in general, highly skilled performers do not have faster simple reaction times than lesser skilled performers.

However, this doesn't mean they don't respond faster. In one conceptualization of how the brain works, an individual's ability to respond to a situation (what scientists call 'response time') is made up of several elements. First is the initial reaction to the change in perceptual information denoting that something new/important has occurred. This is what's capture in simple reaction time. In complex situations, this perceptual information is then interpreted, reflecting the processing time needed to determine what this information means and the appropriate response to it. Once the performer has decided on the appropriate response, they must execute it, which relates to movement time.

Only the reaction time component has been found to be similar between trained and untrained individuals. The other elements of response time vary considerably. As you'd expect, more skilled performers are faster and more accurate at executing their decisions. Furthermore, they can interpret the variety of available perceptual data more rapidly and choose the most appropriate response faster than performers with less skill.

Consider the following example from professional baseball: a Major League Baseball centerfielder has to catch a flyball hit deep and decide what to do next. Do they throw the ball to the pitcher (maybe, but not if there is someone on base who has tagged up and is trying to advance), do they throw the ball to first base to try to tag the runner (maybe, but not if there is a runner at third looking to steal home), do they throw the ball to third in the hopes of holding that player there (very likely), do they hold on to the ball if they are looking to see if additional information emerges that might help with their decision (perhaps, if they had good confidence that their throw to home would beat the runner)? Determining which of these is the correct option takes time and the amount of time depends on the number of decisions involved.

Psychologists William Hick and Ray Hyman studied how quickly individuals could react during tasks with a differing number of choices. These 'choice reaction time' experiments provided the basis for what became the Hick-Hyman law, reflecting the relationship between number of choices/options and the time it takes to make an accurate decision. Essentially, these experiments compared how quickly individuals respond to decisions with varying possible options. Notably, as the number of options doubled (e.g., from two to four to eight and so on), the amount of additional time required was the same (about 150 milliseconds). The implications of the Hick-Hyman law emphasize the value of reducing the number of response options as much as possible (such as when our centerfielder uses his prior knowledge or training to eliminate the options of throwing to first or throwing to the pitcher, thereby reducing a four-choice task to a two-choice). Understanding and maximizing efficiencies in how we process information has since become the foundation of approaches to improving athlete cognition, perception and, thereby, performance. Further, this work highlighted the importance of understanding the role of decision-making, strategy, and other forms of cognition for understanding elite performance. Studying Babe Ruth was just the tip of the iceberg in terms of what science has learned about the psychology and neuroscience of sporting excellence.

Chapter 5. Think (and Train) Like a Grandmaster

In the 1960s and 70s, the United States was gripped with chess hysteria, almost solely the result of a socially awkward genius named Bobby Fischer. Fischer revolutionized the sport in the west, taking the game from parks and smoky coffee shops to arenas, where games were followed around the world. Fischer's rise to fame was meteoric; he won the US Chess Championship at 14 and became the youngest grandmaster in history at 15. At the age of 20, he won the US Championship again with 11 wins in 11 games, the only perfect score in the history of the tournament. Fischer lost his last match at the age of 23 and would not lose another match or tournament for the rest of his life.[50]

In many ways, Fischer was a product of his time. He was the major player in a game dominated by Russian players at a time when tensions between the US and Russia were at an all time high. His time at the top would be defined by constant accusations of Russian collusion and interference (e.g., an article in Sports Illustrated focusing on Fischer was called "The Russians have fixed world chess"), strange demands for the competition venues (e.g., removing television cameras from the 1972 World Championship in Reykjavík, Iceland because they were too distracting), revolutionary approaches to preparation (e.g., he was an early exponent of physical conditioning for chess players, active in tennis, swimming and boxing in the lead up to major competitions) and possible mental illness (e.g., diagnoses of autism, schizophrenia, and paranoid personality disorder have all been proposed[51]*). Bobby Fischer was a chess rock star who achieved the type of celebrity the chess world would never see again.*

In 1973, likely driven at least partially by this monumental interest in chess, two cognitive psychologists conducted a small study at Carnegie Mellon University that revolutionized how scientists investigate exceptional achievement.[52] The first member of the duo was Herbert Simon, already a world-renowned leader in human decision-making and artificial intelligence who would go on to win the Turing Award (essentially the Nobel Prize for computing) in 1975 and an actual Nobel Prize in economics in 1978. He was joined in this endeavour by William Chase, also a psychologist at Carnegie Mellon. While not as well-known as Simon (possibly due to his untimely death in 1983 at the age of 43), Chase made a number of substantial contributions to our understanding of human memory and learning.

Their study is notable for several reasons. It's seen by many as the first study in what would become the field of *human expertise.* Although there were studies of highly skilled performers throughout the history of psychology, there was no field of study that focused on how understanding experts could help us understand not only the limits of human potential but how to design better models of human cognition in general. The study involved only three chess players, one a master-level player, one an advanced-level player, and the other a novice. While a study of this size and design might have a hard time getting published in a scientific journal today, the Simon and Chase study is the first mainstream study in psychology to highlight that experts' ability to process information was domain specific. That said, many aspects of their methodology largely come from the work of a much-lesser known Dutch psychologist, Adriaan de Groot, who conducted landmark studies of chess players' cognition[53]. de Groot, himself a chess master who played for the Netherlands in the 1937 and 1939 Chess Olympiads, spent a significant portion of his research career trying to understand how chess players' thinking and decision-making changed as they became more skilled. In particular, de Groot emphasized the importance of memory for chess performance since he saw the game essentially as a problem-solving task that required utilizing one's memories of similar experiences. His experiments focused on using 'think aloud' methods to understand the decision-making process during critical elements of the game. Interestingly, de Groot did not find many differences in what could be called the 'gross' elements of cognition, such as the number of decisions made, or number of options considered, but higher skilled players were still somehow able to consistently arrive at better moves than their lesser-skilled peers.

de Groot developed a host of innovative approaches in attempts to elicit the expert advantage. The one that captured the attention of Simon and Chase involved a short-term memory recall task. This method goes back to work by Russian psychologists in the 1920s who found that adding elements of 'resemblance to chess' increased the recall of more skilled player.[54] Simon and Chase focused on this element in their experiment, which also involved the recall of chess pieces after short viewing periods. However, to test the value of chess-related structural information on the recall of pieces, they divided the chess boards into those with pieces displayed in structures that made sense in chess play and those where the pieces were just randomly placed on the board (e.g., Figures A and B below). Figure A displays a chess board from a game between Bobby Fisher and another chess genius, Mikhail Tal, at the Chess Olympiad of 1962. The board in Figure B reflects the same number of pieces but randomly positioned.

As expected, given the results from de Groot and his predecessors, more skilled players were able to recall additional information for the structured chess boards but not for the randomly placed boards. To understand the implications of this finding, it's important to understand a bit about what is being tested in those random boards.

In 1956, psychologist George A. Miller published a paper – "*The magic number seven, plus or minus two: Some limits on our capacity for processing information*" – in which he proposed human brains had a fundamental limit to the amount of information that could be held in memory for a short period of time (known as short-term memory).

A

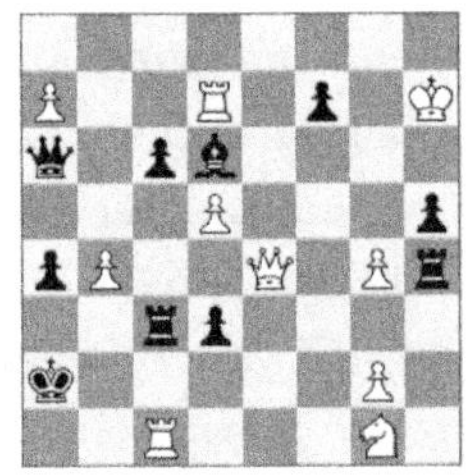

B

When we are presented with lists of items (e.g., numbers, words, etc.), most of us can recall somewhere around 7 items. Miller's proposition in this paper was that human short-term memory span fell between 5 and 9 items (usually 7 but sometimes plus or minus two). Although the actual limits of short-term memory continue to be debated, what is clear is that there is a limit.

By presenting the chess pieces randomly in the unstructured boards, Simon and Chase were testing chess players' short-term memory span, which didn't differ across the skill levels. Therefore, the skilled player's superior ability to recall information had to have something to do with the structure of the information presented because this was the only difference between the tasks. The importance of *how information was structured* became a running theme in much of Simon's research, and a broader theme in cognitive psychology more broadly.

Rather quickly, this focus on information structure trickled down into research in sport. In an early series of studies on athlete perception, Canadian scientists Fran Allard and Janet Starkes explored the capabilities of highly skilled performers in volleyball and basketball.[55] With a high degree of experimental precision, Allard and Starkes dissected the elements of visual skill in both sports, noting the exceptional capabilities of highly skilled athletes were limited to the pickup of information with high relevance to their performance. For instance, in a series of experiments in volleyball, they showed picking up information that was more relevant to performance (i.e., a volleyball) in an image was done much more quickly than less-relevant information (i.e., a referee). Furthermore, they found no differences between skill groups in the speed of identifying generic targets (e.g., whether an image of a country landscape contained a barn).

Subsequent studies built on the assumption that the key to understanding expert athletes in sports like volleyball and basketball, where the quality of an athlete's time-restricted decision-making was an important predictor of success, would not be found in generic tests of general or innate qualities such as short-term memory and reaction time (termed 'hardware'). It would be found through understanding the performance requirements of these sports and how athletes' brains adapt to decidedly unique cognitive demands. In other words, it was in the athletes' 'software'.

Once this argument started to take shape, the evidence in support grew substantially. In a series of studies in the 1980s and early 90s, Australian researcher Bruce Abernethy demonstrated the perceptual and cognitive skills of expert squash and badminton players were highly attuned to the performance demands of their competitive context. The speed of play in these sports has become so rapid it's hard for the average person to comprehend. The fastest strike to date in a racquet sport, for example, was in badminton; Malaysia's Tan Boon Hoeng smashed a shuttle at 417 km/h in the 2017 Japan Open finals. As a result, elite competitors have had to develop highly specific perceptual capacities. In his early studies, Abernethy showed that experts were able to identify key sources of information from their opponents to anticipate their forthcoming actions;

otherwise, the speed of the game is so rapid and the complexity of the response so great, they are unable to respond in time (see our earlier discussion of the Hick-Hyman Law). These sources of information are spatial (i.e., knowing where to look and what to look for) but also temporal (i.e., knowing when this information is important). For instance, expert badminton players use information from the position of their opponent's racquet and arm to predict what action they are going to execute; furthermore, they pick this information up earlier than less skilled players – in some cases as early as a quarter of a second before the racquet comes into contact with the ball/shuttle. In the rapid world of elite sport, this time difference matters.

Since these early studies, the proposition that the perceptual cognitive skills of elite performers are highly specific to their domain of experience has become more and more strongly supported. A recent example is what's called the 'left-hander advantage'. In many interactive sports, left-handed players have an advantage because they are less common than right-handed players. At one point in time, for example, 35% of the top 100 tennis players in the world were left-handed, despite only 10% of the population having this characteristic. The effect is driven by a mechanism known as 'perceptual frequency' – the idea that your perceptual system adapts to phenomena it sees more frequently. If you increase a player's exposure to playing against lefties, the effect usually disappears. Tennis was quick to catch on to this effect and, as a result, the dominance of left-handers has diminished.[56]

As you might expect from this perceptual specificity, the skills that experts acquire to help them succeed in their sport seem to be limited to that domain. Squash players are not much better than novices at anticipating tennis shots, for example. There has been some evidence that very generic elements of information processing transfer but nowhere near the extent of the domain specific effect.

What this work collectively means is that the expert athlete's perceptual and cognitive system is highly specific to his or her experience and performance context. This domain specificity also implies these effects are driven by experiences within the domain of expertise, as we see in athletes' capacity to pick up patterns of structure in domains they see most regularly, but struggle in other domains (e.g., the soccer player trying to predict volleyball attacks) or with less familiar opponents (e.g., left-handers or those with strange biomechanics).[57] The issue then becomes, to what extent can the average athlete acquire these adaptations or are experts predisposed to this development in a way the average person is not.

Without doubt and likely without exception (aside for simple tasks), the time course for these adaptations is extensive. In Simon and Chase's classic study, they note "There appears not to be on record any case (including Bobby Fischer) where a person has reached grandmaster level with less than about a decade's intense preoccupation with the game."[58]

For many psychologists, the work of Simon and Chase (and others) re-focused discussions of human achievement to emphasize the role of training and experience. At the moment, any discussion of talent, development and elite performance undoubtedly includes recognition of the contributions of Anders Ericsson, a Swedish-born psychologist who worked at Florida State University until his death in 2020. More than any other person in the past 40 years, Ericsson revolutionized how we think about and investigate elite performers. In a time when most scientists and researchers work in relative obscurity, Ericsson is renowned as the 'deliberate practice' guy. Over the past two decades, much has been made of the importance of deliberate practice, a very specific type of focused and effortful training. This concept first emerged in the early 1990s, but it wasn't until the mid 2000s that it really started to gain momentum in popular science books and business texts, most notably in Malcolm

Gladwell's mega-best seller *Outliers*. The premise underpinning the notion of deliberate practice is that individuals have a surprising degree of control over their achievements and that exceptional human performances are largely explained by the time an individual spends in high quality, very effortful practice.

The relationship between practice and improvement goes back to the earliest studies in psychology. In 1897, William Lowe Bryan and his graduate student Noble Harter examined the development of telegraph skill– a worthwhile outcome considering the time period, although the telephone was already starting to become widely used.[59] Bryan and Harter's research produced two highly influential papers in *The Psychological Review*.[60] For a while, studies describing the time course of learning proliferated, focusing on relatively simple motor tasks (typing, mirror tracing, or cigar rolling skill) but emphasizing the strong positive relationship between time spent practicing and performance.[61] The relationship between practice and improvement is not linear, however, as anyone who has started a new training program knows. There is rapid improvement at the beginning but gradually these improvements becoming harder to achieve and practice must be increased in order to make comparable gains.

In 1980, psychologists Allen Newell and Paul Rosenbloom proposed the relationship between practice and learning was best fit using a 'power' function (see figure below) while others have argued the relationship is exponential – regardless, the relationship between practice and improvement across the time course of athlete development is not as simple as it might first appear, and as you become more skilled, the amount of work you need to do to keep improving increases considerably.

Ericsson was intimately aware of this work on practice and learning. In fact, during the late 1970s, Ericsson conducted one of the most important experiments in human learning while a post-doctoral researcher at Carnegie Mellon.

The Power Law of Practice

The experiment involved an 'average undergraduate student'. Steve Faloon (known as SF in subsequent publications), had average intelligence and memory abilities and was paid to come into the lab on a regular basis to be part of a learning study that involved practicing a "memory span task for about an hour a day, 2 to 5 days a week, for over 2 years." The basic procedure involved reading random digits to SF at the rate of 1 digit per second, after which he would have to recall the digits back to the researchers in order. If the sequence was reported correctly, the length of the next sequence was increased by one digit. If the recall was incorrect, the sequence's length decreased by one digit. After each trial, SF provided verbal reports of his thought processes during the trial and at the end of each session, he was asked to recall as much of the material from the session as he could.[62]

What is more, the researchers captured the entire learning process through over 250 hours of experimental testing. After starting out at the levels of the average person (~7 digits), SF was able to develop the capacity to recall over 80 randomly generated digits, arguably the most impressive memory feat ever captured in science. What's different about what SF did, compared to other amazing feats of memory such as those performed by memory experts recalling the digits of pi[63], for instance, is the random generation of material at relatively short intervals (1 second). This would be like changing the values of pi each time to make a new sequence of numbers to be recalled.

The researchers were measuring a capacity called 'digit span', which is believed to reflect an individual's capacity to store information in 'working memory' (i.e., your temporary memory storage such as when trying to remember a person's phone number). This capacity is usually positioned as a relatively fixed entity, peaking in early adulthood and decreasing linearly due to age-related cognitive decline. It is not supposed to be as malleable as the SF experiment showed it to be. It's important to note that SF didn't improve his working memory capacity; when he was asked to recall randomly generated letters instead of numbers, his performance went back to normal ranges. Similar to other memory experts, SF figured out a memory trick to help him circumvent the limits of his working memory. It turns out he was a very good runner (a 2:39 marathoner) and developed a mnemonic to convert the random digits into running times. For instance, a 4-1-3-1 sequence could become a mile time of 4:13.1. He 'chunked' the individual pieces of information, which allowed more effective recall of information.

The SF experiment is impressive because of the phenomenal memory feat captured for posterity, but also for what it showed about the value of focused training with appropriate feedback for understanding expert performance. Until this study, it would have been easy to dismiss these astounding performances as anomalies, with little relevance for understanding the average person's performance. SF showed these feats were in the realm of possibility for the average person provided they are able to do the appropriate amounts of the 'right type' of practice.

A key element of the deliberate practice framework, and one that is largely ignored by simplistic summaries focusing on the quantity of practice, is that the *quality* of one's engagement in an activity is critical for maximizing learning and adaptation. Despite the current fascination with deliberate practice, this idea is not new. Some of the earliest psychological studies on learning and attainment highlight a similar relationship. In 1921, one of the most widely used early psychology textbooks notes the following in the chapter on learning:

> Merely repeating a performance many times does not give the high degree of skill that we see in the expert telegrapher or typist. Ordinarily, we practise much less assiduously, are much less zealous, and have no such perfect measure of the success of our work. For "practice to make perfect", it must be strongly motivated, and it must be sharply checked up by some index or measure of success or failure. If the success of a performance can be measured, and chalked up before the learner's eyes in the form of a practice curve, so that he can see his progress, this acts as a strong incentive to rapid improvement. Ordinarily, we have no clear indication of exactly how well we are doing, and are satisfied if we get through our job easily and without too much criticism and ridicule from people around. Consequently, we reach only a moderate degree of skill, nowhere near the physiological limit, and do not acquire the methods of the real expert.[64]

Motivation and effort are central to learning and especially central to Ericsson's notion of deliberate practice. In their initial review of prior research in developing deliberate practice, Ericsson and his colleagues noted the most commonly cited element in studies of effective learning was "the subjects' motivation to attend to the task and exert effort to improve their performance". Impressive effort and motivation are not enough, however. Training in a vacuum, even at the highest levels of intensity, is no recipe for success. In order to optimize training and practice opportunities, developing performers need to have access to high quality instruction. In sport, this comes largely from coaches, but at later, more elite levels of development can also come from subject matter experts such as strength and conditioning specialists, skill acquisition advisors and sport psychologists who can assist in how training stress is applied to gain maximal learning and adaptation. These learning resources are a key element of what makes deliberate practice 'deliberate', by providing the specific areas for the learner to attend to in order to promote their continued development.

The evidence for this approach is very compelling, especially in sport. In a recent review of the literature in this area, our research team noted that in all but one study, top performers differed from their lesser skilled peers on overall hours of training – and in the one study that did not show this effect, a difference was found in time spent doing very specific forms of training.[65] My colleagues and I have explored this concept extensively in sport. Our first exploration was in domains where a high degree of decision-making was important for successful performance. We compared the practice activities of top Australian athletes in basketball, field hockey and netball to a non-expert group of highly experienced athletes from the same sports who had not managed to achieve a very high level of success. By having highly experienced players in the comparison group, we tried to control for sheer length of practice experience. Since nearly all the athletes in both groups had greater than 10 years of involvement in their sports, we could focus on questions like 'how much training did experts do compared to non-experts?' and 'how are the ways experts train different from non-experts?'.

To start the exploration, we focused on measuring the athletes' training history, both in their sport of specialization as well as other sports. For training within their primary sport, we also examined the specific training activities they performed across their career. Researchers, generally, have struggled to capture indicators of practice 'quality' in sport since time spent in training is usually focused on promoting ongoing adaptations to training loads or figuring out ways to turn weaknesses into strengths. Put more simply, all sport training at the elite level hopefully has a purpose and could, arguably, be gauged as high in quality or relevance for improvement.

As expected, more skilled athletes accumulated more training than their lesser skilled peers. However, there were important nuances in the results. First, there was a negative relationship between the sheer quantity of training athletes reported prior to becoming an expert and their exposure to other sports during early development – the more sports they were involved in, the fewer sport-specific hours they needed. Since this initial study, several researchers have found that for some athletes, participation in a lot of different sports early in their careers increased their likelihood of success as adults.[66]

The second notable finding was in the activities that distinguished experts from their peers. As you might expect, experts spent more time in structured training sessions in teams, but they also spent more time in video training and one-on-one instruction with a coach, which they rated as being most important for the development of key performance capacities like perception and decision-making. In addition, experts spent more time in competition, which they rated as being the most important type of engagement for the development of these capacities.[67]

That competition would emerge as a key distinguishing variable was surprising but might be important for highlighting why sport is different from other forms of human performance. Unlike musicians playing in a symphony orchestra or chess players trying to determine the best move in a given situation, sport is inherently dynamic. Researchers have distinguished the difference between 'open sports', where the environment is constantly changing and unpredictable (e.g., soccer, tennis) and 'closed sports', where the environment is relatively stable and consistent (e.g., most running and swimming events, gymnastics).

However, even closed sports are more dynamic and unpredictable than most other activities. For instance, consider golf, one of the most closed sports there is. Among the factors affecting a golfer's play are weather conditions (is it windy, cloudy?), crowd noise (is the crowd for or against the player?), and opponents (is a competitor having a great game and challenging for the lead?). Picture a first chair violinist playing outside in a windstorm to an unruly crowd while a competitor for their seat is actively playing against them, and you get some idea of the performance-related differences between sport and domains like music. From this perspective, it is impossible to replicate the demands of sport competition in the training environment; this can only be done in competition.

Much of the work on the role of focused training and deliberate practice has been restricted to sports requiring a high degree of decision-making and anticipation. Certainly, the most compelling evidence in support of this very nurturist perspective on human development comes from activities with a high degree of learning and cognition. In the early 2000s, my colleagues and I investigated the value of this type of training for a sport where performance was less about cognition and more about physiological workload. We chose to examine the role of deliberate practice in groups of Ironman distance triathletes. The Ironman triathlon involves a 4km swim leg, a 180km cycle leg and a 42.2km running leg. Most serious triathletes consider completing the Ironman a rite of passage and qualifying for the Ironman World Championships held in Hawaii each year as the pinnacle achievement in the sport.

Like the Australian decision-making project, we were interested in the types and amounts of training done by triathletes at different levels of skill and performance. Unlike that project, where we struggled to find clear ways of classifying athletes into skill groups, triathlon has an objective performance standard which allowed us to create groups of male triathletes who were performing at the 'front of the pack' (the top 5% of performers), those in the 'middle of the pack' (around the average time) and those at the 'back of the pack' (the bottom 5% of performers).[68] The advantage of studying triathlon is the three disciplines are primarily aerobic activities, which means you can create a very crude estimate of the overall training load performed by each athlete over time. First, we did this by approximating the total numbers of hours each athlete spent in organized training for swimming, cycling, and running. This included time with a coach, training with a squad, training alone and so on. Most of these athletes were in their early 30s so this often involved tracking training activities going back over two decades. As expected, top competitors put in significantly more training than the other two skill groups. In fact, they put in twice as much training (an average of 12,500 total hours in swimming, cycling, and running) compared to competitors finishing in the middle of the pack (~6200 hours) and over three times more training than those at the back of the pack (~4100 hours).

On the face of it, total training time seems like a good predictor of where you end up in terms of finishing performance. It's important to note, however, that these totals were averages across the groups. This is critical because there was significant overlap between the groups. There were members of both lower skilled groups who had done *more training* than members of the elite group. Similar findings are echoed in other research on differences between skill levels in the quantity of training.[69] Total hours of training seems to be a key variable for understanding differences between groups of performers, but it loses some of its power as an explanation when you compare individual to individual.

This is the difficulty with trying to solve an immensely complex problem like explaining elite performance with a single solution. In general, the number of hours spent in training is a vital predictor of skill level and more practice will lead to better performance. Differences between groups of performers, whether they are chess grandmasters compared to beginners, or Olympic champions compared to those at the back of the pack, are largely explained by time spent in practice. However, when comparing individuals within a population of athletes, there is a high degree of variation. The message: '*all other things being equal*, your ability to design and accomplish more high-quality hours of training has a large effect on your eventual performance' is reasonable and defendable. However, things are never equal.

Chapter 6. Winning the Biological Lottery

In 2004, Markus Schuelke, a physician and scientist working at the University Medical Centre in Berlin and his colleagues published a brief report in the New England Journal of Medicine on a "Myostatin mutation associated with gross muscle hypertrophy in a child".[70] The report detailed the case of a young child who exhibited markers of neurological disfunction shortly after birth. Upon further examination, the attending physicians noticed the newborn was 'extraordinarily muscular, with protruding muscles in his thighs and upper arms'. While the neurological issues seemed to resolve themselves after a couple of months, follow up with the child continued at least until the age of four and a half years, due to the extreme muscularity. Examinations revealed the child had a rare mutation in the gene for a growth factor called myostatin. In normally developing children, this gene controls the growth of different types of tissues in the body. If this growth is uninhibited, which is what seems to have occurred in this young boy, advanced muscularity occurs. This phenomenon is not as rare as you'd think. Certain breeds of cattle are known for their increased muscularity, which is shown to be due to myostatin regulation. Similarly, a breed of whippet in dogs called a 'bully whippet' looks like the canine equivalent of a body builder.

The applications of this type of mutation for sport performance are obvious, as is what they seem to tell us about the role of genetically-related factors for other aspects of human health and development. For instance, could regulation of myostatin hold the key to muscle wasting diseases like muscular dystrophy? Since this case report in 2004, the potential of myostatin – at least as a direct influence on human function and performance – hasn't paid off. After promising results in animal models, trials on humans with forms of muscular dystrophy showed no improvement in either pediatric or adult samples.[71] While the role of genetic factors on human development is unquestionable, precisely how they affect performance, learning, and other developmental outcomes is complicated.

Our understanding of the role of genetic factors on human performance and achievement has a long history, tracing back to the original work by Francis Galton. Galton's initial work in this area focused on 'family studies' based on the correct assumption that family units would share transmissible information from one generation to the next in a way that non-family relations would not. He was also a strong proponent of the study of twins; even before we understood the unique biology of identical twins (monozygotic, referring to when one egg is fertilized and then splits in two) and fraternal twins (dizygotic, when two eggs are fertilized by separate sperm), Galton had the insight that they might help us understand the roles of nature and nurture.

At the same time researchers in cognitive and sport psychology were producing evidence in support of the role of the learning environment in understanding human expertise, researchers in biology and physiology were having their own breakthroughs. The most important of these, undoubtedly, was the publication of the human genome in 2001. 'Undoubtedly' because of what it showed us about the role of biology in understanding who we are, but also for what it didn't show us. In conceptualizing the Human Genome Project, estimates put the number of genes in our genome at around 100,000 protein-coding genes, but when the first estimates from the project came out, this number was reduced to somewhere between 20,000 and 25,000, although the actual number is still not known.[72] Moreover, much of the material in our genome is 'non-coding' meaning that it has no specific role in creating the proteins related to biological development or functioning.

Given that we have fewer genes than initially thought, we could think this would place a premium on the genes we have. It turns out, similar to the case with myostatin mutations, things are more complicated. Part of this complication comes from confusion about what key terms mean. Take the word 'gene' for example. As the cognitive psychologist Steven Pinker notes in his essay "*Why nature and nurture won't go away*" the word 'gene' has had a range of meanings during the twentieth century including "a unit of heredity, a specification of a part, a cause of a disease, a template for protein synthesis, a trigger of development and a target of natural selection".[73] For our discussion on the role of genes for human performance, we'll focus on genes as the part of chromosomal DNA that produces a functional protein (i.e., something that leads to or influences a biological outcome).

Another commonly used term is 'heritability'. This is what reporters are normally talking about when they say, 'science has shown insomnia (or personality, or religiosity, etc.) is genetic'. There's much to unpack here. First, our individual genes produce the proteins that drive any adaptation, learning or change, and so in that sense everything is genetic. What they mean is the genetic differences between humans are related to why some people have insomnia (or certain personality characteristics, or are more religious, etc.) and others don't/are not. This might be related to specific direct relationships between genes (e.g., in the traditional Mendelian sense taught in many high school biology classes) or indirect relationships where genes relate to other behaviours or outcomes that are linked to insomnia (e.g., people with certain personality types or who behave in certain ways before going to bed may predispose themselves to increased likelihood of suffering from insomnia).

Second, when a research study or social media headline says '50% of personality is genetic' this doesn't mean half of *your* personality is genetic. Heritability is only relevant to understanding variation in a population. It has limited relevance for understanding individuals. The '50% of personality is genetic' finding means in a given population, half of the variation between individuals can be explained by differences in genes.

Sequencing of the human genome has found individuals are more than 99.9% identical in their DNA profiles.[74] This less than 0.1% difference is enough to explain the variation, at least the variation related to genetic differences, between us. The genetic raw material that makes up each individual is known as their 'genotype'. This is different from the eventual manifestation of a behaviour or trait that a person displays to the world, which reflects their 'phenotype'. For instance, an individual might be biologically predisposed to be tall (their genotype) but whether that above average height translates into exceptional skill in basketball, volleyball, or changing light bulbs (their phenotype) depends on how these genetic predispositions interact with the resources and pressures in the environment the person finds themselves in.

Genetic differences between all of us are explained by differences in base pairs, the chemical elements that connect to each other via the opposite DNA strand in the classic double-helix structure. Estimates are that we have ~3,000,000,000 base pairs in our genome, with millions of potential genetic variations between individuals.[75] In humans, the most common genetic difference is when one base pair varies, known as a single nucleotide polymorphism (an SNP, commonly called 'snips').

A number of snips have been associated with aerobic and anaerobic performance in humans as well as their risk for injury and response to training.[76] In addition to these more physical variables, there have been a number of snips associated with cognitive function such as reaction time, impulsivity, working memory and attentional control.[77]

One of the first 'candidate genes' to emerge for sport performance involved a polymorphism in the gene for ACE, an enzyme involved in controlling blood pressure and fluid-electrolyte balance. Given this involvement, it made sense that ACE would have a relationship with athletic performance, particularly in endurance sports where cardiovascular function is important. Initial examinations of endurance athletes ranging from Olympic rowers and Ironman triathletes to high altitude mountain climbers suggested that as aerobic endurance requirements increased, the proportion of the sample with the beneficial markers for ACE also increased.[78] However, despite the early promise of research in this area, replication and, more importantly, prediction, proved difficult in subsequent studies.

Another early, and ultimately more promising marker was found in the ACTN3 gene, where a snip related to muscle composition and function hypothetically predisposes individuals with different forms of this gene to better performance in either power or endurance activities. Over the past two decades, results in this area have been more consistent; a recent review of studies on this gene by Olympian and geneticist Craig Pickering argued one specific polymorphism was related to improvements in strength and injury prevention, noting it goes beyond simply being a 'gene for speed'.[79]

Other polymorphisms in specific genes have been proposed, but despite the early excitement in this area, most genetic researchers have generally moved away from this type of analysis for understanding the role of genetics on sport performance. The likelihood of single snips paying off in a big way for complex outcomes like sport performance is small. The evolutionary biologist and geneticist Richard Lewontin dismissed this process of identifying these types of markers for complex outcomes as the 'search for a single gene as magic bullet approach'. The sheer number of potential genes and polymorphisms in the genome increases the likelihood of finding 'false positives', which explains why many promising genetic markers did not replicate in subsequent, better designed studies. Second, apart from well-known genetic diseases (e.g., Huntington's disease, Duchenne's Muscular Dystrophy), which affect a single area of the genome, the norm is that human characteristics are robustly 'polygenic', that is, they are determined by multiple genes working in elaborate and interactive ways that are highly dependent on environmental effects. Importantly, the polygenic nature of most forms of human performance and function mean that if you don't have one type of beneficial genetic marker, you can make up for it by having a different, similarly beneficial, genetic marker. A 2008 study by geneticists Alun Williams and Jonathan Folland explored the likelihood of having 23 beneficial markers for endurance performance, estimating the odds of one person having all of the markers was 0.0005%. The authors noted, "As the number of DNA variants shown to be associated with human endurance phenotypes continues to increase, the probability of any single individual possessing the 'preferable' form of each polymorphism will become even lower."[80] While research hasn't replicated several of the genes, the lesson remains – not having a specific genetic marker may not be a big deal.

The reality is that even simple outcomes are enormously complicated from a genetic standpoint. Height, for instance, is related to *hundreds* of genetic variants in approximately 180 different locations on the chromosomes.[81] Eye colour appears even more complex.[82] All this to say, the characteristics and behaviors involved in sport performance and athlete development are considerably more complex than these types of candidate-gene approaches assume. As neuroscientist Kevin Mitchell noted in a recent Twitter thread "genetics…is not about genes causing traits. It's about how 'variation' in genes causes 'variation' in traits".[83]

To return to our example of the infant with the myostatin mutation, this alone is not enough. The whole approach – that single genes affect single outcomes – is flawed for several reasons. First, genes don't work independently, and the reason the child with the myostatin mutation is unlikely to succeed even in a sport or other domain where increased muscularity is critical, is because it's only one gene in a complex polygenic system. In order for this increased muscularity to be beneficial it would need to be supported in the right ways by other elements of the body, such as stronger connective tissues (e.g., to prevent ligament and tendon damage from greater muscle mass and the resulting force production[84]).

Second, the capacity to take advantage of the genetic differences depends on the developmental ecosystem in which the athlete is placed. Early thinking about the role of nature and nurture on development used some form of the 'bucket analogy' – that nature determines the size of the bucket and nurture controls what goes into the bucket. This metaphor is too simple, incapable of capturing the complexity of the interaction between these broad categories of influences. A better metaphor, proposed by evolutionary biologist Richard Dawkins (among others) is to see human development and achievement like a cake, which starts out as a set of raw ingredients that, when placed in the appropriate environment becomes a delicious cake, but placed in the wrong environment becomes something else entirely. As science journalist Matt Ridley noted in his 2003 book *Nature via Nurture*:

> The processes involved in behavioral and psychological development have certain metaphorical similarities to cooking. Both the raw ingredients and the manner in which they are combined are important. Timing also matters. In the cooking analogy, the raw ingredients represent the many genetic and environmental influences, while cooking represents the biological and psychological processes of development.[85]

At no point is it possible to divide the cake back into the component parts isolated at the beginning.

The obvious role of the environment is presented in great detail in other fields of biology. Botanists, for example, are able to take clones of the same plant and raise them in different environments to determine the influence of factors like elevation or hours of sunlight exposure on growth. Similarly, physiologists can procure animals with specific genes 'knocked out' of their DNA, which allows them to more precisely explore the function of these genes in isolation (e.g., by comparing between animals with and without these genes). Typically, this is done in mice, but the advancement of technologies like CRISPR[86] suggests this will soon be possible in other animals.

What makes this more complicated in humans, particularly those participating in sport, is that many aspects of our behavior are voluntary, driven by an individual's desire to satisfy basic needs (enjoyment, competence, social connection) through this behavior. Athletes, even very young ones, aren't like plants or mice who can be dropped into an environment without considering how that environment 'fits' with the desires and needs of that individual. We cannot simply impose external motivation on someone and expect them to persist in their engagement in any meaningful way, certainly not over the time course needed for high level skill development.

Based on this complexity and the noted flaws in prior designs, more sophisticated approaches to identifying the genetic characteristics underpinning sports performance have been developed. Genome-wide association studies (GWAS), for example, are becoming increasingly common. This approach does not require any theoretical rationale for the pre-selection of genetic variants and instead analyzes a large number of snips (usually greater than a million) in a single analysis. This type of analysis is 'hypothesis free', which results in it having the flexibility and freedom to explore novel variants. This is important in a field where our understanding of genotype-phenotype interactions is so incomplete. Despite the promise of this approach, its relevance for sport settings may be limited, at least at the moment. Genome-wide analyses are expensive to conduct, and the potential for false positives, simply due to the large number of comparisons being performed in the analysis, requires enormous samples (usually tens of thousands of participants).

While cost is a real obstacle to this type of research, the real barrier is sample size. For instance, consider the UK's 100,000 Genomes Project, launched in 2012. The research focuses on sequencing the entire genomes of over 100,000 individuals. This is the size and scope of study designs currently being undertaken. However, if we start to parse the number of individuals who are 'sporty' we can quantify the size and scope of the problem. First, let's assume the 100,000 individuals were a random selection of the UK's population. If we consider a general adult sport participation rate of 36% in the UK population (~41% of male adults and ~32% of female adults report participating in sport at least once a week), if we wanted to examine genetic predictors of forms of 'sport engagement' our sample would be limited to 36,000 (i.e., since 64,000 reported no sport engagement). As we sub-divide this group further, the sample is reduced considerably. If we focus on football/soccer, ~3% of the UK population participate in this sport on a regular basis, which reduces our number down to 3000 individuals before sub-dividing further by gender, age or skill level.[87] The role of specific genes is inevitably confounded across different sports, sexes, and age groups. Perhaps most powerful are the impacts of different skill levels. High-performance cohorts are, by definition, rare. In one discussion of defining skill groups, a quantitative classification identified the most elite performers as being two standard deviations from the average performance, which means for every 1000 performers in a sport, only 3 would meet the criteria for inclusion. Of the individual genomes targeted for the 100,000 Genomes Project, this suggests only 9 of the 3000 UK football players *might* meet the requirements for a study of elite football players.

Furthermore, given the 'rabbit holes' many researchers and practitioners found themselves going down in the 1990s and early 2000s with candidate genes like ACE, many are preferring an approach of "analyze, replicate, repeat" before making any firm conclusions. Another approach involves de-emphasizing the meaning or importance of any single study so that statistical requirements around sample size can be loosened, resulting in the greater likelihood of studies with 'null effects' and/or exploratory analyses being published. This would allow smaller studies or those with more elite samples to make their way into the scientific literature, which allows them to be identified and used in approaches like meta-analyses and systematic reviews that synthesize the results from all studies in an area to make more robust conclusions. Here, the time course for determining what an individual study 'means' has to wait until it can be considered relative to other work in the field.[88]

That said, a number of GWAS effects have replicated consistently, revealing associations that may be relevant for understanding athlete performance and development. For instance, a 2017 meta-analysis of GWAS studies revealed several relationships between genetic markers and indicators of general cognitive function,[89] a finding that was corroborated by a 2018 GWAS that implicated over 500 genes as playing a role in differences between individuals on this outcome.[90] GWAS has also been used to explore differences in measures of sleep quality and duration[91] as well as indicators of personality[92]. The relationships between these outcomes and athlete development or performance are probably highly nuanced – the right profile is likely necessary for elite performance but not sufficient to explain differences between those who are successful versus unsuccessful at the highest levels. Furthermore, looking for 'a' profile of genetic influences excludes the more likely possibility that there are multiple patterns that may lead to eventual sporting success, a notion we return to in a later chapter.

Publication of the human genome emphasized the problematic simplicity of our approaches to how genetic raw material ends up producing the complexity we see in human populations. However, these simplistic attitudes persist among many laypeople, especially in sport. Genetic testing is regularly discussed among coaches and other athlete development support staff, usually from the perspective of 'how can knowledge of genetic markers help us design better training?' rather than as prescriptive assessments for talent identification and selection. Despite these discussions, it appears genetic testing is not widely used, at least at the moment. This will likely change soon. A recent paper noted that among those who were not currently using these types of tests, the most common reasons were lack of awareness and/or considering the tests too expensive.[93]

Because of their potential to be used in destructive ways, the prevalence of 'direct to consumer' genetic testing has led to clear directives from the scientists leading this work. A 2020 update from the International Federation of Sports Medicine[94] once again (as they did in 2015 and 2017) noted this type of testing was ill-advised. More forcefully, they argued that "given the polygenic nature of athletic performance and sports skill, talent identification or selection of optimal sports by using only limited genetic variants is unlikely ever to be a possibility".

The back and forth, tug of war between nature and nurture has done much to mask the realities of what this simplistic view of talent means for our understanding of human accomplishment, and, more importantly, for the athletes who aspire to sporting greatness. It is important that coaches, athletes, and other stakeholders move away from the notion of genes as direct mechanisms for athlete development. If they have any role in athlete development, they do this through a complicated interaction with athletes' environments, which makes it very difficult to conceptualize and measure, at least with the simplistic approaches used to date.

It is also critical that sport stakeholders do not take this to mean genetic factors are irrelevant to the art and science of coach and athlete development. Genes may play a key role as 'necessary but not sufficient' elements in the development of skill and performance. This might explain the mixed results in previous work; there is limited variability in these elements in the population because only athletes with these characteristics are still in the system, which affects the usefulness of statistical tests requiring variability within samples being compared. Despite our propensity to want to view the world as a series of simple cause and effect relationships, there is still considerable 'noise' influencing outcomes throughout development. While this perspective recognizes the key influence of the environment, it also re-positions the role of genetic factors from being 'deterministic' to being 'probabilistic', where certain combinations of variables might increase an individual's likelihood of success but there is still flexibility and variability in how this success actually occurs.[95]

Section II: Compromising Greatness

In truth, there is compelling evidence found on both sides of the nature-nurture debate. The value of training and experience on achievement and development is unquestionable, as are inter-individual differences in genetic factors, many of which are linked to variables essential for success in different types of sports. The fact that those in either camp can credibly argue from a position of strong evidence means something is wrong in how we've framed the question of human attainment.

This is not just a semantic issue about how researchers do their job. The emphasis on talent and its early identification has important implications for those participating in organized sport. This section focuses on the process of athlete development, the elements that help it go right and the ones that help us understand when it goes wrong.

Chapter 7 focuses on the power of being labeled as 'talented' or 'not talented'. Because the long-term engagement in practice is critical to skill development, and the foundation of this engagement is continued interest and participation, these labels have the potential to undermine the entire process. This is followed, in Chapter 8, by an exploration of how youth sport has changed over the past few decades, affecting the types of developmental environments athletes engage with during critical early periods. The concept of early specialization, the current villain in discourse about early athlete training, gets special attention. Chapters 9 and 10 explore two pillars of the mythology of sport, the first is the idea of sport as a meritocracy, where everyone has equal potential for success, and the second is sport as an overwhelmingly positive environment for human development. The final chapter in this section (Chapter 11), focuses on the issue of talent in professional sport. Collectively, these chapters highlight the limits and opportunities in how sport is currently structured and delivered.

Chapter 7. The Power of Labels

In 1935, Austrian physicist Erwin Schrödinger proposed a paradox to try to understand an elusive component of the burgeoning field of quantum mechanics, namely how an element of a quantum system can exist in multiple states (e.g., as a wave and as a particle) at the same time. The gist of the experiment goes like this: imagine a cat living in a closed chamber. In the chamber is a vial of poison, a Geiger counter and a small amount of radioactive material. If the radioactive material is detected, the vial of poison is broken and the cat dies.[96] *Here's the crux of the paradox, the amount of radioactive material is so small there is a 50-50 chance of it being detected. At any point in time, you do not know whether the cat is more likely to be alive or dead. It's not until you open the chamber and actually observe the cat that you can make this determination - until then it's technically alive and dead, a state physicists refer to as a 'superposition'.*

At its most basic, managing and maximizing human potential is the primary objective of athlete development systems; however, the reality is, in many sport systems, this objective is of secondary concern, if it's considered at all. Few coaches, parents or administrators contemplate the human costs of an athlete development system that emphasizes early talent assessment and selection. Despite this lack of interest, better management of the potential of young athletes will inevitably become more important as the landscape of sport changes.

The warning signs are there if you know where to look. Rates of youth participation in all forms of physical activity, including sport, continue to dwindle over time, ultimately affecting the size and fitness of the pool of athletes for development (among other serious social and personal health consequences). Further, research on skill acquisition and expertise is very consistent in its emphasis on the long-term nature of this process, at a time when sports are making selection decisions earlier and earlier in development. The limited understanding of the process of long-term skill acquisition and the poor accuracy of our talent selection decisions means we're removing young athletes from development systems precisely when we should be trying to keep as many as possible, for as long as possible.

If we stretch Schrödinger's paradox a bit (okay, quite a bit) to the context of sport, imagine a young athlete involved in an organized sport program. Up until this point, she's received no explicit feedback on whether the system sees her as talented or not-talented – she is essentially in a state of superposition, having both talent and no-talent at the same time. It's only after an external agent 'observes' her talent (or lack thereof) that she ceases being one and becomes the other.

We have very little understanding of the consequences of this observation but they're likely profound. In the field of gifted education, for example, one of the rare, early studies found children who are considered by their parents as less gifted report lower self-esteem and higher anxiety than their more gifted siblings.[97] This seems reasonable given that our perceptions of self-esteem and self-worth are regularly grounded in social and peer comparisons. Given how regularly these types of decisions are made in youth sport, it's remarkable how little we know about their effects. Researchers have tracked the long-term development of those who stay in the system, but haven't explored how this implicit 'you have talent' message affects athlete motivation and enjoyment. It's reasonable to assume being told you are talented is beneficial for developing and sustaining motivation, but the relationships are undoubtedly more complicated. For example, one of the organizations I worked with a few years ago described a unique problem they were facing with junior national team members. The athletes were so satisfied with being identified as good enough to make their junior national team that they stopped striving for excellence (i.e., they felt that they'd 'made it' and didn't need to work hard anymore). This intriguing effect may partially explain the low conversion rates reported in team sports between athletes who play on junior national teams and those who end up making it to the national team.[98]

Understanding the relationships between values, interests, motives, and behaviour is one of the most complicated areas in psychology. Even more complicated is trying to capture how these relationships change over the protracted time required for long-term skill development. We simply do not understand the types of motives that are best suited for long-term perseverance in elite sport or how these motives change across an athlete's development.

That said, the issues noted above fit with several general approaches to motivation. Attribution Theory[99], for instance, focuses on how individuals explain the causes of their successes and failures. Do they attribute success to others (e.g., "I'd like to thank God for this victory today") or to their own hard work? A key distinction is whether the perceived cause is external (due to factors outside my control) or internal (due to factors related to me). This distinction relates to something referred to as the 'locus of causality' – do you see the reasons for your success or failure as resulting from your own actions/inactions or through the influence of someone else? An additional element of attributions that is especially relevant in performance settings is whether you see these influences as stable (unlikely to change in a future situation) or unstable (likely to change in the future).

Our beliefs about talent (i.e., believing you either have it or you don't) are internal and stable factors since most, nearly without exception, see talent as something stable across time and development. This can be maladaptive since it de-values personal contributions to success, such as better management of training effort and recovery, largely by undermining the 'locus of control' (i.e., whether you perceive that you have control over your future performance).[100] This notion of personal control also shows up in Self-Determination Theory, currently one of the dominant theories of human motivation.[101] This theory places a premium on feelings of autonomy – the degree to which you feel in control of your behaviour and the likelihood of attaining future goals. Labeling an athlete as talented or non-talented emphasizes elements of development that may remove that individual's sense of agency and autonomy over their destiny. As a result, it might undermine behaviours like practice and recovery that are critical predictors of long-term development.

Complicating things further is the reality that not all athletes who eventually succeed do so in a smooth, clearly delineated path, where their 'talent' was immediately obvious and nurtured. Human development is rarely that simple and clear. More often than not, it's messy, complex, and difficult to predict.

One intriguingly 'messy' group involves athletes who receive negative competence feedback (e.g., being deselected from their team) but don't drop out of sport, eventually managing to develop into an elite performer. Michael Jordan being cut from his high school basketball team is the best known example. Most models of motivation struggle to explain these types of results since the relationship (a negative assessment leading to a positive effect) isn't intuitive. Although we have no idea how common this is, anecdotal and qualitative reports indicate some athletes take this negative feedback in a way that leads to the development of key psychological skills that end up positively affecting their long-term attainment.

Over the past 10 years, there has been increasing attention to the idea that what many would call 'negative life events' often have positive effects on athlete development. Although there had been some discussion of the role of challenges and discomfort in prior work on positive youth development, mental toughness and resiliency, the interest and intensity around this issue became magnified in 2012 with the publication of "*The Rocky Road to the Top: Why Talent Needs Trauma*" by sport psychologists Dave Collins and Aine MacNamara.[102] In this position paper, the authors argued that deliberately removing obstacles from athletes' lives is counterproductive for the development of the types of psychological skills necessary for future success. As the authors note "the talent pathway should not be a comfortable place to be" and forward-thinking administrators and coaches should include "structured trauma designed and implemented as part of the [talent development] pathway".

In my experience, many practitioners have struggled with the word 'trauma', mis-interpreting it in a way that makes the discomfort or challenge more severe than originally intended. Future work by Collins, MacNamara and their team has clarified that the types of 'trauma' advocated for athlete development systems is 'minor harm or impairment' necessary to "facilitate the training, use, and refinement of fundamental psycho-behavioral skills and confidence to deploy them, thereby, facilitating optimal development".[103] While considerable work is necessary to provide clear guidelines for those working with athletes, what seems clear is that the process of athlete development requires a degree of challenge and adversity that was not well considered in much of the prior work in this area.

In other areas of human development, researchers have emphasized the importance of seeing youth as 'antifragile', a concept originally developed by statistician Nassim Nicholas Taleb in his 2012 book *Antifragile: Things that gain from disorder*.[104] Anti-fragility reflects the reality that many key skills cannot be developed in the absence of challenge and discomfort, a concept that is emerging as crucial for understanding human development and coping, particularly in contexts like sport. Anti-fragile systems are different from resilient systems in that they require challenge or difficulty in order to improve. The best example of anti-fragility is our body's immune system, which requires exposure to new viruses and germs in order to defend against more significant threats. Living in a germ-controlled environment that limits the body's exposure to minor level pathogens seems to be a perfect recipe for disaster when exposed to more serious agents. In a similar way, seeing athletes as antifragile and providing them with opportunities to work through challenging situations, positions them as better able to respond to and overcome the novel 'threats' they'll experience in the variable and unpredictable contexts of elite competition.

There are many other elements in the vast unknowns of athlete development. For instance, while we have some, albeit limited, information about how and why some athletes remain in the system and eventually succeed, we know considerably less about those who drop out of the system. Based on the limited information we have, it's reasonable to suspect that part of their decision to withdraw was driven by negative feedback about competence or a lack of enjoyment, but much of this is speculation.

There are also important distinctions between groups of athletes who drop out of sport. Those who drop out due to lack of enjoyment, negative feedback or too much pressure, reflect an understandable and predictable relationship – the sport experience led to a de-valuing of sport over time. However, there is another group of athletes who receive positive feedback about their competence but still drop out of the system. We know essentially nothing about this group, nor how common an occurrence this is.

The low rates of conversion from junior national to senior national teams in many sports[105] could simply reflect changing interests across human development. We often ignore, or at least under-appreciate, that sport training does not happen in a vacuum; throughout their development, athletes have varying interests competing for their time and attention. It may simply be sport is not meeting the fundamental desires and needs of the athlete at that time, ultimately undermining their potential for long-term success.

Clearly, the psychological ramifications of ascribing someone as having talent (or not) are complicated. Moreover, the impact of this message can vary from athlete to athlete based on the quality and breadth of their social support network (e.g., peers, parents), how the message is framed, and/or the types of opportunities left for the individual to continue participation. Despite these potentially negative and long-term costs, athlete selections will still be required due to limited resources such as highly qualified coaches, top-tier training facilities, and so on. A minority of athletes will continue to receive better supports and training environments, gaining developmental advantages that compound themselves over time, while a majority train in lower quality settings or disengage altogether. And so it goes.

How do we improve a system that, paradoxically, seems to be aware of its limitations (although perhaps not the full extent of the costs of these limitations) but continues along seemingly without much interest in improving? If anything, things may be getting worse – at least as reflected in news coverage about the negative impact of sport participation on brain injury, athlete mental wellbeing, and a host of other developmental outcomes.[106] Moreover, how do sport stakeholders advocate for a system that emphasizes the positive impact of participation (e.g., development of self-esteem and confidence) while acknowledging the very real negative aspects that can come from an over-emphasis on early engagement and talent selection?

Despite some strong rhetoric in this area, it almost certainly does not reflect apathy or cynicism on the part of those working in the system. By and large, sport stakeholders are intimately aware of the limits of their systems. In philosophy and ethics, scholars have noted what they term the 'Principle of Double Effect' - when commission of an act, while legitimate and well-intended, leads to a negative effect that would normally be avoided. In medicine, issues related to abortion and euthanasia are 'double effect problems' since all solutions lead to some negative consequence.

In psychology, the 'Trolley Problem" is a series of thought experiments where individuals have to consider ethical decisions about whether to sacrifice a small number of individuals to save a larger number. The basic setup goes like this:

> A trolley is barreling uncontrolled down a set of railroad tracks. Up ahead, five people are tied to the tracks with the trolley heading straight toward them. You are standing next to a lever that can divert the

> trolley to another set of tracks and away from the group of five. However, if you divert the trolley you will kill a single person standing on the other track.

What is the most ethically defendable solution? Do you simply do nothing thereby allowing the trolley to kill the five people on the main track or do you divert the trolley onto the other track where it kills one person? There is no solution in which harm is unavoidable and the issues are more nuanced than you might expect (e.g., in one scenario you have direct 'agency' over the outcome because it requires an action from you). Psychologists and philosophers have used this thought problem to explore moral and ethical thinking since it was first proposed in the 1960s.

Sport is rife with variations of the trolley problem. Coaches and scouts are aware of the negative consequences of the selection decisions they make, and undoubtedly aren't comfortable with these decisions for many athletes, but they still need to make them. There simply isn't enough space to keep everyone in the system given its current resources. To make things more complicated, coaches have to juggle what might be best for an athlete's long-term development (e.g., providing an environment that might build intrinsic motivation slowly over time) with short-term needs (e.g., winning their league or regional tournament). Many coaches' jobs depend more on short-term success than on the number of athletes they develop over the long term.

When a policy advisor decides to advocate for the use of limited sport funding for high-performance sport instead of grassroots programming, or when a coach picks players to create a team with the greatest chance of short-term success over players with higher potential for developing into superior performers in the long-term, they are dealing with variations of the Trolley Problem. The same occurs when a professional team manager chooses one superstar player over 2 or 3 lower-level players for the same amount of money.

These types of problems, where choices result in 'wins' in one area but losses in another, are common in sport, and reflect a type of

'Kobayashi Ramu' situation (after the famous 'no win scenario' faced by Captain Kirk in Star Trek II: The Wrath of Khan). All choices lead to negative effects somewhere, and these questions highlight the difficulties and complexities faced by many sport stakeholders working in a typically under-resourced system.

The trolley problem helps us understand the subtle and not so subtle effects of selection on factors related to athletes' long-term development. After an athlete receives feedback on whether they do or do not have talent, there may be effects on motivation, desire, interest, and enjoyment, among other important outcomes, simply through this message. Human beings are fundamentally motivated by drives to demonstrate competence. It's why we generally continue doing things we're good at and tend to stop doing other things. Popular concepts like the need for 'self-determination' are grounded in the notion that our need to feel competence drives behavior (as well as satisfaction, connection and enjoyment).[107] Further, applying a label of 'talented', or focusing too much on talent identification, undermines the agency necessary for development.

The one, very clear conclusion we can make from the last decade of research conducted in this field is that we undoubtedly underestimate how complicated and difficult the task of athlete selection is. Researchers in this area get incredibly frustrated when critics note 'well it didn't work in situation X'. It is no hard task to cherry pick examples of where talent selections have gone wrong. What's amazing, given the complexity of the task, is how often it looks like coaches and scouts get it right. Most of the time, however, this too is likely an illusion, demonstrating our capacity to quickly embrace evidence that confirms our beliefs over contrary evidence that challenges them.

Most approach this problem as if it's a simple question with a binary response – is this person talented (yes/no), and accuracy is evaluated based on whether this was the correct decision.

	Correct Decision?	
Talent	Yes	No
No talent	Yes	No

However, this seemingly simple question is profoundly more complicated than this. Consider the next series of questions in terms of how this decision plays out across the time course of athlete development. Our assessment of whether this athlete has talent is largely based on the characteristics they are demonstrating at this moment in time and, therefore, any athlete identified as talented will be demonstrating 'early talent' since those with the potential to demonstrate 'later talent' are not viewed in the same way, and are likely not selected. A more advanced approach to selection would look at athletes as demonstrating early talent, the potential for later talent, which is not yet demonstrated, or, no talent.

	Correct Decision?	
Early Talent	Yes	No
Later Talent	Yes	No
No talent	Yes	No

This distinction between indicators of early talent and talent that is yet to emerge (later talent) is critical given the low predictability of early indicators in many sports, and the difficulties of those with potential for later talent staying in the system after being deselected. The complexity doesn't stop there though. We also need to consider whether this selection was the right thing for the athlete's development (e.g., is an athlete best served by being on a junior national team and travelling to gain experience or is it better to stay home and focus on training consistency?) *and* whether he/she were then moved into an environment that was optimal for his/her continued development.

	Correct Decision?		Right Environment?	
Early Talent	Yes	No	Yes	No
Later Talent	Yes	No	Yes	No
No talent	Yes	No	Yes	No

What this 'optimal environment' encompasses is complicated. It involves access to high quality coaches, supportive peers, skilled opponents and the like, of course; but there is a subtle complexity to how an individual athlete responds to different situations. For example, in the Great British Medalists project, an athlete's capacity to experience an early traumatic life event and use it as an opportunity to develop resiliency and mental toughness was linked with something positive that was currently happening in his/her sport.[108] Despite all we know about optimal environments for short-term learning, our understanding of optimal environments for long-term development is limited.

These questions and limitations are then added or multiplied with the number of selections that occurs in an athlete's sport across his/her development. In the image below we've noted a 4-step selection process, but it's rarely this infrequent across an athlete's development. Consider competitive ice-hockey in Canada, for example, where players have to try out for spots on a team every year of their engagement starting at least as early as the atom level (9-10 years).

	Selection 1				Selection 2				Selection 3				Selection 4			
	Correct Decision?		Right Environment?		Correct Decision?		Right Environment?		Correct Decision?		Right Environment?		Correct Decision?		Right Environment?	
Early Talent	Yes	No	Yes	No	Yes	No	Yes	No	Yes	No	Yes	No	Yes	No	Yes	No
Later Talent	Yes	No	Yes	No	Yes	No	Yes	No	Yes	No	Yes	No	Yes	No	Yes	No
No talent	Yes	No	Yes	No	Yes	No	Yes	No	Yes	No	Yes	No	Yes	No	Yes	No

This isn't only an academic argument; it's a mathematical one. Consider in our image above that for an athlete to make it successfully through this hypothetical 4-step process, they need to accumulate 'yes' in each of the appropriate columns (i.e., 8 positive responses), which emphasizes the far greater likelihood of selectors, coaches, and athletes to get it wrong than to get it right.[109] Trying to identify the right person for the right environment at the right time rapidly becomes an exercise in futility, but such is the world of elite youth sport – at least in a system of athlete development based on assumptions that early selections are credible and accurate assessments of youths' long-term potential for success.

Importantly, we haven't yet raised the issue of chance or luck and how it affects long-term development. Jack Coles works as a 'recruitment analyst' for Leicester City FC's academy in the UK, and has a wealth of examples of how serendipity affected professional players' eventual success. On one occasion, he describes a player who turned up for pre-season practice but accidentally joined in with the first team instead of reporting to the U18s training session as instructed. The first team manager was new and none of the players questioned it. In the training session, he blew everyone away due to his pre-season fitness (he was a cross-country running champion). The team manager kept him with the first team from then on. He now plays for a Premier League club.

Then there was the youth playing for Northampton Town who missed the text from his coach telling him he wasn't needed for the away game that weekend. The player showed up as the bus is leaving and the manager decided that since he's there, he may as well come with the team. The player ended up playing the last half hour due to another player's injury and did so well he stayed with the team for the rest of the season. He now has a professional contract, also in the Premier League. It's impossible to quantify or predict these types of serendipitous events, but they likely have a larger impact than we think on whether an athlete makes it or not.

These examples reflect the considerable amount of 'noise' interacting at any given time, emphasizing that we had better be confident in the labels we place on developing athletes. As previously noted, nearly everyone begins with the potential for improvement if they keep practicing, but without the proper motivation and drive, extensive practice doesn't happen. This is one of the problems with an over-emphasis on deliberate practice as the single explanation for exceptional sporting achievement; in the long-term time course of expertise acquisition, engagement in practice is both an effect and a cause.

This is the basis of the 'growth mindset', the notion that focusing on personal accomplishment from a position of 'growth' is more adaptive for learning and development than seeing these as the result of fixed factors such as talent.[110] Although the power of this effect may be overstated[111], there are important 'takeaways' about the importance of exploring multiple solutions for why some succeed and others do not.

Similar notions to 'mindset' exist in various forms across the field of sport psychology and motor learning. For instance, motor learning scientists Gaby Wulf and Rebecca Lewthwaite frame the opposing ways of explaining skill development as reflecting an 'inherent ability belief' which sees skills as largely unchangeable, or an 'acquirable skill belief' where abilities are seen as changeable through experiences such as attention to high quality training. Like the research on mindset, findings reveal that how we think about our own abilities matters because they a) influence our attributions for success and failure and b) affect our behaviour toward or away from the activities that actually matter.

Studies of youth, for example, have shown those who hold inherent ability beliefs about athletic performance are more likely to have maladaptive motivational profiles, as reflected in focusing too much on winning or attributing performance to innate characteristics rather than training and persistence, compared to peers who saw performance as reflecting acquirable skills.[112] Similarly, believing athletic ability is fixed and innate is associated with negative or helpless reaction patterns, such as higher levels of anxiety, decreased levels of satisfaction, and 'self-handicapping', a strategy used to protect one's self-esteem in situations involving social evaluations.[113] This latter finding may be most important since how you think about abilities and attainment affects how you approach problems related to skill development. If you believe skills and abilities are the result of practice, then you are more likely to spend more time practicing. Likewise, believing them outside of your control can undermine the motivation to spend time practicing in order to improve.

Holding beliefs that explain your performance as the result of your hard work and persistence are more 'adaptive' in different settings, which facilitates continued engagement and effort. Motivationally, athletes with acquirable skill beliefs are more likely to focus on personal improvement and mastery of the task. Instead of focusing purely on whether they won or lost, the key question is 'did I improve?'. They also report higher levels of enjoyment and satisfaction with their engagement in training and competition. Perhaps as a result, they spend more time practicing, have greater self-efficacy and confidence, and obtain better learning effects over time.[114]

Although our understanding of how these beliefs develop and persist is very limited, they seem to be highly malleable, at least in the short-term.[115] This suggests coaches and parents can affect these beliefs through the messages they provide. Comments like 'you're so good at that' versus 'that might not be the sport for you' differentially affect competence beliefs and can steer an individual's motivation toward or away from the activity. These messages can be influential, and we need to be more aware of the messages we're giving (either implicitly or explicitly) to athletes. This may be particularly important during early phases of development when extrinsic feedback and social support may be more instrumental for learning and skill acquisition. Furthermore, given the process of skill acquisition in most sports, anything that undermines the development of key psychological elements at the foundational stage may be particularly detrimental to the likelihood of long-term success.

Chapter 8. Will There Ever be Another Dave Winfield?

In Toronto, the city where I work, Dave Winfield will always be remembered as the player who helped the Toronto Blue Jays win the 1992 World Series against the Atlanta Braves - that, and being the player who killed a seagull with an errant throw while playing for the Yankees in 1983.[116] *After a storied career with the San Diego Padres and New York Yankees (and short stint with the California Angels), Winfield was picked up by the Jays in 1991 as a designated hitter, hitting .290 with 26 home runs.*

Despite only having one World Series win over his 22-year career, Winfield is widely considered one of the best ballplayers of all time. A case could also be made for him being one of the best athletes in history in any sport. After playing both baseball and basketball at the University of Minnesota (including helping the school win Big Ten Conference championship in both sports), Winfield is one of only three athletes in history to be drafted by 4 professional leagues (the NFL, NBA, ABA and MLB).[117] *Amazingly, Winfield was drafted by the Minnesota Vikings in the 17th round of the NFL draft despite never playing football at the high school or college level!*

Like other areas of human development and attainment, the seeds of future sporting success are planted early. Discussions of athlete development over the past decade have almost invariably mentioned the ongoing trend towards early specialization. Although the definitions of when this occurs and what this entails vary across studies, it generally reflects young athletes focusing their sporting experience into a single sport. As one would expect, this can lead to concerns about the pressures and stress being placed on young athletes. For instance:

- Focusing in a single area limits the breadth of physical stress on developing young athletes, presumably leading to over-loading particular areas of the developing musculoskeletal system. At the same time, specialized training usually increases the overall quantity of training stress occurring in a phase of development. This *increased depth* of training coupled with *decreased breadth* is linked to over-use injuries.[118]
- A specialized approach to training limits the number of activities youth are participating in which may reduce opportunities for the development of what are referred to as *fundamental movement skills*, considered the necessary building blocks of lifelong, healthy movement.[119]
- Although research in this area is sparse, what limited work there is suggests restricting opportunities for social interaction during youth is related to lower social and emotional development.[120] This fits with other work which suggests breadth and quality of social experience in youth and adolescence is important for healthy development.[121]

Despite the clear significance of these developmental consequences, it is important to acknowledge the evidence base in this area is plagued with inconsistent definitions, poor measurement precision, problematic study designs and a general lack of critical thinking about what these findings mean for athletes and sport systems. To be sure, there is strong rhetoric around early specialization; however, we have very little knowledge of the mechanisms driving these effects. Several position statements are grounded in the speculation that specialization *might* influence these outcomes without establishing the causal evidence chain to prove it. Like many areas of youth sport, simply identifying the effect is not enough to be able to solve it. We need to understand the mechanisms to be able to alter training environments, sport policies and parent/athlete behaviour.

It is also important to anticipate the implications of policies and consensus statements painting early specialization as the villain of athlete development. Most families do not have the time nor financial means to place a child, let alone multiple children, into several sports. Policies and models that argue for, or moralize this as a necessary step for developing expertise, could disadvantage those at the lower ends of the socioeconomic spectrum, compounding already notable socioeconomic biases in participation.[122]

Notions of 'sampling' and 'diversification' as more beneficial forms of engagement for youth athletes may be phenomena from a bygone era. Sport systems have changed over the past two decades and the days of youth participating in multiple sports in a largely play-based and unorganized fashion are likely over, at least without massive re-structuring of not only the sport system, but society in general. Despite the trend towards the nostalgia of the 'good old days' when we think about youth experiences in sport and play, there is evidence indicating the extent to which things have changed. For instance, data from a series of US studies tracking how youth spent their time since the 1980s indicated decreases in 'discretionary time' (i.e., time spent in activities of the youth's choosing, such as unorganized play) and increases in more structured forms of activity such as organized sports.[123] Youth also spend more time with their parents then they did a few decades ago. The data on changes in social media use over the past decade (and their implications for youth development) are even more startling.[124]

Establishing the risks of early specialization requires data from as contemporary a sample as possible since data from past samples may be, at best, irrelevant and, at worst, misleading. In sport contexts, unfortunately, there haven't been many studies of how training behaviours of competitive athletes have changed over time. However, the change in *how* training is delivered during early development is far-reaching. Later in the athlete development pathway, it is likely highly trained athletes run up against a threshold of the amount of absolute training that can be done and the amount of recuperation time necessary to recover and adapt from that training. Ericsson's early work on deliberate practice suggested a daily limit to the hours of highly focused, effortful work a person could do in a given day.[125] This daily limit hasn't really been explored fully, but let's agree that there is likely some threshold of load that an athlete can handle before exhaustion or injury, and that this varies by individual. Later in development, this load is delivered in highly organized and intensive ways, via experienced and qualified coaches, trainers and the like – through an organized and highly connected support team. However, early in development this training load can be delivered by coaches who may not be fully equipped to understand the importance of how and why to balance training experiences.

Single-sport engagement and specialization do not have to be synonymous. Instead of glamourizing the past – an ineffective strategy since we do not definitively know what was so great about the past in the first place – a more fruitful approach would be to figure out why early specialization leads to these negative consequences. For instance, is the mechanism too much intensity too early, or too much pressure on winning leading to decreased enjoyment and motivation, or lack of opportunities to develop fundamental movement patterns which leads to increased injury risk? All of these are possible mechanisms (among others) and while it's likely a combination of these factors, each is modifiable in a single-sport training environment. Understanding the mechanism is critical.

Another limitation of prior work on specialization is that it has been treated as if it's the wrong end of a dichotomy (specializer or diversifier/sampler) when it is more accurately a point on a continuum of sport engagement. In this simple continuum, specialization and diversification are anchors, reflecting the poles within which the training experiences of a future elite athlete are captured. To illuminate, let's anchor athletes at each end with roughly the same level of achievement. On the specialization end, the best-known example is arguably Tiger Woods, who is famous for his early devotion to practice, appearing on the Mike Douglas show at the age of 2.[126] To anchor the other end of the continuum, I propose Babe Didrikson-Zaharias. With all due respect to Dave Winfield's accomplishments discussed at the opening of this chapter, Didrikson-Zaharias is arguably the greatest athlete of the past century, if not the entirety of human history, and the best model for multisport engagement in existence. Babe grew to prominence in track and field. In 1932, she attended the US Olympic Trials in Evanston, IL, competing in eight events and winning the team championship *despite being the only person on her team*. The year prior (1931), she led her women's basketball team to an AAU championship. She is the only person, male or female, to win Olympic medals in running, throwing and jumping disciplines (setting four world records at the 1932 Games). Didrikson-Zaharias also competed in basketball, tennis, baseball and pool (among other sports/activities), but her greatest success was in golf. Over a 20-year career, she won 41 LPGA events including 10 majors. One newspaper perfectly described her as operating "like a woman whose life is a constant campaign to astound people." Indeed.

With our continuum in place (the Didrikson-Zaharias/Woods scale), we can discuss the patterns of engagement that can lead to optimal learning and development for long-term success. One obvious difference between the careers of these two exceptional athletes is the years they were active (1930s-1950s for Didrickson-Zaharias and 1990s-2020s for Woods). As discussed, the ecosystems of different sports have changed significantly over this time, so a logical question is whether these changes have made it more difficult to diversify one's sport involvement (e.g., is it easier to be a Tiger these days than a Babe?). Similarly, could Babe have become Babe if she followed a Tiger-like trajectory and vice versa?

These questions sit at the heart of the debate about specialization and diversification. If it is more difficult to diversify one's involvement in the current sport system, the relationship between diversification and achievement, noted in several recent studies, highlights an important flaw in how we deliver coaching and support throughout the athlete's journey to greatness. Moreover, if diversification of engagement is more difficult, a critical question becomes 'how does this difficulty relate to eventual success?'

Again, socioeconomic status could explain the relationship between diversification and success; those who are able to participate in greater and more varied sport experiences are more likely to be successful. While it would appear that the engagement pattern is the reason for success, in reality this correlation simply reflects the collective benefit of greater socioeconomic status. The cumulative power of socioeconomic advantage is so great that it directly or indirectly influences all of the so-called 'social determinants of health'.[127] Amazingly, there has been very little examination of the power of socioeconomic variables in explaining sport attainment. The limited research that has been done suggests socioeconomic status affects the potential of someone participating in sport in the first place, but may not be related to the likelihood of making it to the highest levels of sport more generally. Analyses from a large-scale study of Canadian and Australian athletes found family socioeconomic status did not predict differences between the skill groups. More simply, once you're already in sport, richer parents do not necessarily make you more likely to succeed.[128]

Anecdotally, parents and athletes have also reported that the demands of participation in a single sport, at a competitive level, have increased over the past few decades. Although there isn't a lot of tracking research on how athlete training has changed over time, we may have enough to suggest the following:

Training requirements have changed. Interestingly, there seems to be very little research tracking how athletes use their time in training, and whether the content of an athlete's day (e.g., training, recovery, leisure, sleep) is measurably different today than it was in decades past. That said, there is some research indicating approaches to training have changed. As noted earlier, from a learning perspective, training design has evolved to focus on ensuring training stimuli are more 'representative' (i.e., training demands mirror competition demands). Similar results have been found in the few tracking studies of physiological workload. Two tracking studies of Norwegian rowers[129] and Dutch speed skaters[130] generally show a movement towards training becoming more systematic and targeted over time.

Costs of participation have magnified. There's been limited research tracking the costs of participation in youth and high-performance sport. That said, there are publicly available sources that highlight the extent of the changes over the past few decades. In their exploration of the costs of participation in youth ice hockey in Canada, *Selling the Dream,* Ken Campbell and Jim Parcels noted the increasing proliferation of private primary and secondary schools catering to parents with NHL dreams for their sons. Costs, including room, board and tuition can range over $30,000 per year.[131]

Competing demands have changed. While sport continues to be the most popular organized activity for youth, its dominance in the lives of youth and adolescents may be a thing of the past. In their book, *The Coddling of the American Mind*, researchers Greg Lukianoff and Jonathan Haidt make a strong case for the uniqueness of the current generation of youth, largely because the proliferation of the iPhone has fundamentally changed youth development. It's easy to assume the elements of sport that have made it attractive for youth in the past are equally relevant now, but that doesn't reflect the reality that the social environment current youth are developing in is unique. Social media, video games, and other transformations in how youth spend their time are having, and will continue to have, repercussions throughout the sport system.

Sporting systems and approaches that worked in the past may not have the same relevance in a 21st century developmental context. Things have changed, in many ways dramatically.

Discussions of the perceived value of diversification also ignore over a century of research on the role of practice for improving skill. There are obvious advantages to focusing on the traits/skills that you're eventually going to need in your sport, especially in popular, highly competitive sports like soccer. The critical question then becomes, can we take what we've learned about the costs of this specialized approach to make the journey healthier and more beneficial for developing athletes without these costs?

Let's first consider the proposed risks of early specialization, most significantly the risk of increased injury due to inappropriate balance between training stress and capacity to adapt (i.e., 'too much, too soon'). If we look at athlete training load from this perspective, we, unfortunately, know very little about the hard limits of what the body can handle across development. Moreover, recent research on effort and intensity has emphasized the clear perceptual elements of this phenomenon. Put more simply, athletes perceive workloads differently based on cognitive and psychological states.[132]

Further, given the genetic influences on adaptation and learning, it is likely that clear guidelines, at least for generic training prescription (do stimulus X to attain response Y leading to adaptation Z), are never going to be possible. Some will be able to handle more training, some less. Some will progress more quickly in learning, some more slowly. There will always be a high degree of individual specificity to training design.

So, how does this help us manage any legitimate risks associated with sport specialization? Again, a greater understanding of the mechanisms of learning and performance would be helpful. For instance, in addition to knowing very little about the causes of negative outcomes from specialization, our understanding of the mechanisms by which diversification presumably positively influences skill development is also limited. Is multisport engagement a superior form of engagement because it provides important diversity and breadth of movement exposure, or is it an illusion of superiority because it simply decreases the sport specific load that leads to increased risk? If we return to our Tiger-Babe continuum, there is a lot of real estate between these two poles and therein likely lies the answer for understanding the optimal balance of focused, specialized training relevant for skill development and the broad-based, high variability engagement best suited for development of more general skills and capacities.

If further exploration identifies the optimal balance of activities in early development, the mechanisms are likely linked to research examining how capacities developed or learned in one area can benefit performance in another. In psychology this relates to a field of research focusing on 'transfer of learning', a concept going back to the earliest days in the field.

Edward Thorndike, considered one of the fathers of educational psychology, proposed that any transfer between activities was limited to areas that shared 'identical elements'.[133] These elements can be found in a variety of distinguishable categories. For instance, 'movement elements' refer to the biomechanical and anatomical actions required to perform a task, such as the movement similarities between throwing a baseball overhand and an overhand serve in tennis. Similarly, shared 'perceptual/cognitive elements' could relate to the type of environmental information individuals interpret to make performance-related decisions. For instance, field hockey and soccer both require participants to rapidly assess and recognize patterns of offensive and defensive structure in order to anticipate their opponent's forthcoming actions; therefore, these sports share this perceptual element. This type of offensive and defensive structure would differ in a sport like volleyball and, therefore, the degree of transfer would be reduced. Sports also share 'conceptual elements' such as strategies, guidelines, and rules regarding performance. Gymnastics and diving share conceptual elements (e.g., similar rules), as do basketball and netball (e.g., similar strategies/tactics).

Although not normally a focus in psychological studies, a 'physical conditioning' category should be added to this list of transferable elements. Physiologists examining the effects of 'cross-training' have provided support for the notion that general cardiovascular effects can be transferred, and effects are more likely to occur between sports that share similar modes of activity than between dissimilar modes of activity (e.g., greater transfer occurs between running and cycling, which share similar muscle groups than between running and swimming).[134]

Similarly, psychological elements like the ability to manage and cope with performance pressure, persevere through difficult times, set manageable goals and structure one's time to increase the likelihood of success, may transfer between domains. Indeed, much of the social appeal of sport as an avenue of 'positive youth development' is based firmly on the assumption that elements learned and developed in one context (i.e., sport) transfer to others (e.g., education, the workforce, etc.).[135]

The window for these types of transfer undoubtedly changes across development and throughout training. For instance, consider the physiological changes that occur during an endurance training program. Improvements in aerobic performance involves central adaptations (e.g., increases in blood volume, amount of blood pumped per heartbeat and the maximal output of the cardiac system) and peripheral adaptations to training stress (e.g., increases in the density of capillaries in the circulatory system, density of mitochondria in cells and the amount of activity in certain important oxidative enzymes). The value of cross training for improving aerobic performance appears greatest at the start of a training program because during early stages of training performance improvements are the result of the equal contribution of central and peripheral adaptations. Later in development, for highly trained individuals, these changes are still reflected in central adaptations (e.g., increased maximal stroke volume and cardiac output) but they result from highly specific peripheral adaptations such as the redirection of blood flow away from non-exercising tissues.[136]

If we explore this notion a bit more fully, the benefits of more diversified training being limited to early in development fits with much of the research in this area. For instance, the vast majority of retrospective studies and stage-based models of athlete development note that even athletes with the most diversified pattern of early engagement, shift to specialization as they get closer to the highest levels of attainment. Although it may be plausible that a more varied sport engagement could eventually lead to similar (or even greater) effects, the issue becomes one of time. It isn't possible to gain the same rate and degree of adaptation and learning from more general forms of training compared to more specific forms.

Creating the 21st century equivalent of Dave Winfield requires acknowledgement that sports systems, the athletes within those systems, and the cultural milieu those systems operate within, have all changed, often in profound ways. If the odds of another Dave Winfield are low, how do we need to change the way we think about sport, athlete development and training? How do we manage these issues relative to greater awareness of athlete mental health, wellbeing, and the consequences of an unmitigated emphasis on training quantity? A first step would be to understand the limits of our current approaches and reveal how uneven the playing field really is. We shift our focus here in the next chapter.

Chapter 9. Matthew Effects

One of the reasons the deliberate practice approach was immediately embraced is that it perpetuates a form of the 'Horatio Alger Myth', coined from the series of popular novels written for young boys in the mid- to late-19th Century. Horatio Alger wrote over 100 novels, as well as hundreds of poems, short stories, essays and songs. Although the content of, and audience for, his work varied, he is best known for his 'rags to riches' novels for youth, which typically involved a young boy starting out destitute or impoverished only to gain a position of standing by the end of the book. This myth focuses on youths' ability to rise above his or her stations through hard work and persistence, a notion that pervades the social fabric of countries like the United States, where children are taught that "anyone can grow up to be president". Not everyone bought into the myth - Mark Twain famously lampooned the Horatio Alger Myth in his 1879 short story "Poor Little Stephen Girard". But this notion of 'pulling yourself up by your bootstraps' persists. Interestingly, in Alger's novels the protagonist's success is usually attributed to 'luck' or 'serendipity' rather than hard work.

On its surface, the idea that 'talent doesn't exist and your destiny is in your hands if you just practice hard enough' would seem to be a positive and important philosophy for a society to hold. Who doesn't want to feel in control of their own achievements? From a motivation standpoint, it engages the individual's sense of personal agency in the completion of their goals and emphasizes the internal and changeable elements of attribution theory discussed in an earlier chapter. These are all good things for engaging short-term motivation to practice, work hard, and goal setting.

From a long-term perspective, however, there are troubling implications to this message. Not all individuals are equally positioned to achieve greatness, due to differences in innate capacities, yes, but more so due to variabilities in access to important resources, and biases in how talent is assessed and measured. Although we might all aspire to greatness, some are more likely to achieve it. Despite what attribution theory tells us about the importance of focusing on things that are within our capabilities to change, the playing field is not level and never has been.

Unfortunately, the rhetoric around, and misunderstanding about, deliberate practice has likely ruined the long-term prospects of many developing young athletes, as parents and coaches push them harder and harder based on the assumption that their development, learning and performance are limited by them not working hard enough.

While the mechanisms of sustained engagement are predictable (e.g., enjoyment, feelings of competency, social connections[137]), they are misleadingly complex. Feelings of enjoyment, for instance, come from a range of sources, as do positive social connections. Moreover, while social connections and enjoyment may be somewhat universal motives of human behaviour, where connection and enjoyment come from varies by individual (what elite athletes find enjoyable, you likely would not) and over time (what you enjoyed when you were young is likely not the same things as you enjoy now).

Reductionist approaches to achievement in sport (and other domains) that explicitly or implicitly condense this amazingly complex process into a simple 'sound bites' – '*all you need is 10,000 hours of deliberate practice*', or '*don't specialize*' – mask an important reality of athlete development - that often the flexibility and capacity to take advantage of what seem like obvious opportunities are not under our control.

In 1968, sociologists Robert Merton and Harriett Zuckerman developed what became known as the *Matthew Effect of Accumulated Advantage*. They noted that in science, eminent researchers get more credit for their discoveries than lesser-known scientists even when their discoveries were similar. This leads to a compounded advantage for the more eminent scientist, who is more likely to obtain resources for further research (less teaching, more discretionary time, greater research support). The effect has been shown in a range of domains and situations. In language acquisition, for example, growing up in a house with more books or where more words are spoken is related to greater reading and language proficiency.[138]

Matthew Effects also have a range of influences on athlete development, largely because of relationships we've already discussed - access to things like better coaching and facilities promotes opportunities to accumulate time in superior forms of practice in better constructed learning environments, and these have accumulated benefits over time.

This notion of access to resources as a key factor in promoting future success is foundational for understanding the extensive process of athlete development. Positioning high quality practice as the key component of long-term skill acquisition means any obstacle to this practice disadvantages athletes with more obstacles while advantaging those with fewer. Obstacles to development include a host of seemingly innocuous variables that end up affecting long-term development in a myriad of ways. On the one hand, these obstacles can have immediate effects on athlete development like the way broad indicators of social class (e.g., education levels, income) affect engagement in sport in the first place; higher educational attainment of parents equals a greater likelihood of their kids participating in sport. On the other hand, other factors, like access to superior coaching and instruction, have persistent effects on athlete development, such as when better coaching during early training (e.g., when placed on a 'talent development team'), leads to increases in skill development, resulting in greater likelihood of being placed in better training environments, playing against stronger opponents, and getting further opportunities to access limited resources.

In his book on Matthew Effects in science and education, Daniel Rigney proposes a distinction between what he calls *absolute* and *relative* Matthew Effects. In a fixed resource system, an absolute effect comes when one group (the advantaged) gets 'richer' while another group (the disadvantaged) gets 'poorer' because the resources are delivered disproportionately between the groups. In sport, the notion of 'poorer' is a difficult one to contend with since athletes can continue to develop in the absence of a resource-rich environment. However, one example is when a group of young athletes tries out for limited spots in a local league. Those who are selected get 'richer' compared to their peers who started the selection process with them, while those who are not selected are denied the opportunity.

Relative Matthew Effects are when both groups continue to improve but the rate of improvement in one group is superior to that in the other. In sport, the effects of improved learning and training environments act as a form of 'compound interest', increasing over time and paying off in the long run. This type of effect is more common, and effects tend to cluster together. Higher quality coaching is tied to better facilities, superior opponents and teammates, and greater opportunities for training adaptations. These effects pervade the ecosystem of high-performance sport, ultimately undermining the efficiency of athlete development and any legitimate search for those with the greatest potential for future success because potential is confounded by opportunity.[139]

Consider the 'birthplace effect', a phenomenon that has been noted in a range of international research published over the past two decades.[140] It's grounded in the proposition that areas that differ in key geographic indicators (e.g., population size, density and makeup) disproportionately produce elite performers due to the importance of these indicators for promoting development.

Although the work exploring the impact of geography on athlete development and success is sparse, this distinction has a long history in other areas of human health and social wellbeing. Most census assessments, for instance, use a distinction between 'urban' (high density, lots of resources for residential and commercial use) and 'rural' (often simply referring to anything not classified as 'urban'). Even this simplistic division has revealed robust differences between segments of a population suggesting that broad measures of health, development and function are influenced by an individual's developmental ecology.[141]

The hypothesis that geography can influence development can be traced at least as far back as the late 1800s. In 1888, Arthur Conan Doyle of Sherlock Holmes fame presented a report "On the geographical distribution of British intellect" in a British literary periodical called *The Nineteenth Century*. According to his analysis, major cities had a greater proportion of intellectual activity compared to the country, and agricultural areas were superior to manufacturing or mining areas. Further, success in the arts (e.g., poetry, art, music) was more likely to come from those living in the south, while greater achievement in science and engineering was more likely to come from those living in the north.[142] A similar analysis (in method, not quality) in the United States was undertaken by politician and historian Henry Cabot Lodge in 1891.[143]

In 2006, in an attempt to understanding the broad influence of geographical factors on elite athlete development, I was part of a research group that examined the population of hometowns of athletes in the NBA, NHL, MLB and PGA compared to expectations based on the distribution from the general population, noting that players were more likely to come from smaller cities rather than large cities or small rural areas.[144] When examined at the national level (i.e., the entire country as a whole), this and subsequent studies in sports in North America and Australia generally displayed a 'sweet spot', where medium-sized areas over-produced elite athletes in professional sports like basketball, ice-hockey and golf, while smaller rural areas and large urban centers under-produced them compared to what would be expected.

Further investigations noted that effects were less stable in provinces of Canada with fewer inhabitants compared to more populated ones, undermining the overall assumption that population was a reliable proxy for whatever developmental factor promoted these effects. In that context, the popular and appealing notion of a population 'goldilocks' zone might be a red herring. That said, the assumption underlying the effect (i.e., differing environments have differing influences on attainment) is reasonable even if we do not yet know the precise mechanisms responsible. In Denmark, for instance, a developing athlete's distance from their nearest elite team affects the probability of them attaining professional standing in soccer.[145]

Unfortunately, the role of geographic variables in promoting and understanding human attainment has not been widely considered beyond this sort of simplistic analysis (e.g., comparisons of differences between regions of different size or population density). In other areas, especially health and education, more sophisticated approaches have been developed that use large datasets to determine relationships between geographic indicators and socially-relevant variables (e.g., educational development, indicators and predictors of health and function). This type of systematic analysis of geographical influences is one approach to capturing how social and cultural factors affect athlete development. Nonetheless, the limited evidence we have indicates geography may play an important role in athlete development, likely at various levels.

In much sport research, there is a tendency to conclude 'all barriers are negative and therefore must be removed'. The influence of these barriers, however, is certainly more complex than originally assumed. Take, for example, the Relative Age Effect, which has been popularized in books such as *Outliers* and *Superfreakonomics*.[146] This effect (actually a series of subtly different effects[147]) reflects an annoyingly persistent bias in many sports that results from the use of a standardized 'cutoff date' to group youth into age cohorts.[148]

On the face of it, this is a good idea, since provision of instruction and peer-to-peer competition should be somewhat equalized among individuals at the same levels of development. However, simply using an arbitrary date to regulate who goes into what age group does not ensure equity in how instruction is delivered. Moreover, in the earliest phases of development (e.g., early levels of sport engagement or early grades in school) there are clear developmental differences between individuals placed in the same cohort. For instance, if we consider the commonly used cutoff date of January 1st, a child born on that date will be placed in the same age group as a child born on December 31st of the same year, despite them being a year apart in biological growth and development, not to mention learning and experience.

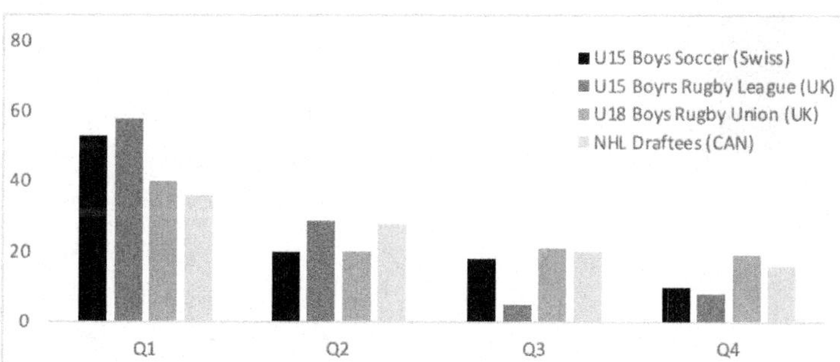

Relative age effects amongst 4 popular team sports. The pattern of results emphasizes the greater likelihood of participation and attainment in the first 3 months after the sports' cutoff dates (Q1) with generally decreasing proportions in subsequent quarters of the year.

The figure shows results from several studies of relative age effects in popular team sports, where some of the largest effects have been seen.[149] These differences are most pronounced in early phases of development and learning; the difference between the oldest and youngest in a one-year cohort of 5-year-olds is ~20% of their chronological age and overall life experience. This difference shrinks as players develop (e.g., the relative difference in chronological age is only ~10% between the relatively oldest and youngest 10-year-old and ~5% in 20-year-olds) but the effects of these differences persist, undeniably due to the lasting influence early success and positive feedback has on motivation, persistence, and skill acquisition.

It would be easy to dismiss relative age biases as quaint little effects, demonstrating the subtle influence of policy and administrative decisions on athlete development. However, the effect has been amazingly persistence over time, in the face of enormous awareness and initiatives to remove it from sport systems.[150] One thing that makes the relative age effect so fascinating and compelling is the emerging work suggesting the developmental benefits to some relatively younger athletes (i.e., those who were initially disadvantaged) if they are able to stay in the system. Several studies have noted relatively younger athletes obtain higher salaries in professional soccer, are drafted earlier into the National Hockey League, and have longer careers than their relatively older counterparts.[151] On the one hand, this may simply reflect that at the end of the athlete development pathway, relatively younger players still in the system have more, or are more homogeneous for, 'talent'. This would explain how they are capable of playing with peers who are more developed than they are during early periods of development, as well as how they eventually obtain higher status (i.e., the 'cream always rises to the top' explanation). A counter proposal would be that playing in environments with stronger, faster, and more powerful opponents and teammates (i.e., the relatively older) promotes greater skill development for those relatively younger players who don't get discouraged and quit, or get cut (i.e., the 'initial disadvantage as eventual advantage' explanation). It is likely a combination of both elements, but regardless, the fact remains – the way Matthew Effects influence development and success is complicated.

One of the most strongly supported hypotheses for why Matthew Effects have such stubborn and long-standing consequences on athlete development is because they have a key role in providing or limiting access to the element that really matters: training quality. It's worth repeating – any factor that affects access to high levels and amounts of training ultimately ends up affecting likelihood of success.

The deliberate practice framework, with its focus on practice quality and learning opportunities, ultimately ends up emphasizing the importance of resources for understanding human development and potential. These types of 'Blank Slate', empiricist approaches, where individuals are encouraged to ignore or overcome biological limitations, do not level the playing field. Instead, the 'equivalency of potential' argued for in the deliberate practice framework relegates these types of Matthew Effects to being trivial or not existing at all. Instead of empowering individuals to take control of their destinies, ignoring these barriers compounds the inequalities between individuals, further compromising their likelihood of success. When access to resources is positioned as critical for understanding development, inequalities in access are magnified, not reduced.

The interactions among these types of social, cultural, and personal variables have implications for the sport system as a whole and it's in sport's best interest to reduce these disadvantages. Apart from the obvious implications for fairness, equity, and equality, if the skill level of the overall population gets better, because barriers to entry and/or development are reduced, the performance of those at the far end of the distribution should also improve. Allowing more people access to sport at all levels (i.e., raising the floor) should inevitably result in better performers emerging at the elite level, as those capable of reaching these levels find and stay in the sports they are best suited for.

Chapter 10. The Price of Glory

In his first Olympics, Michael Phelps finished a respectable 5th in the 200m butterfly event –at the age of 15. Over the next 4 Olympic Games, Phelps would win a total of 28 medals. In addition to holding the record for most overall medals won by a single athlete, he holds the records for most Olympic gold medals (23), Olympic gold medals in individual events (13), and Olympic medals in individual events (16). Over the course of his swimming career, Phelps set 39 world records. At the 2008 Beijing Games, he broke Mark Spitz's record by claiming 8 gold medals in a single Olympics – a record that had stood since 1972 and one many thought would never be broken.

Michael Phelps is the very definition of an elite athlete, by nearly every account the most successful Olympian ever. Lesser known are the mental and psychological issues he experienced during his development. The signs and symptoms were there - DUI charges in 2004 and 2014, a viral video of him using a bong in 2009 – but few saw them as reflecting the difficulties he was experiencing. Research on athlete mental health has exploded over the past decade and currently focuses on trying to understand the distinction between factors that might be requirements of this type of elite performance (selfishness, narcissism, momentous personal sacrifice) and the consequences of this journey (substance use and abuse, difficulties transitioning out of sport). These issues aren't trivial, despite the positive image sport enjoys for most participants. At their extreme they can be life threatening. In an interview prior to the Rio Games when Phelps was at the peak of his status he describes "I had no self-esteem. No self-worth. I thought the world would just be better off without me. I figured that was the best thing to do -- just end my life."[152]

Greatness and expertise hold special places in our society. The compositions of Mozart or Bach, the mathematical and creative insights of Newton or Einstein, and the movement dexterity and fluidity of LeBron or Serena highlight the absolute limits of our potential. In addition to the status they hold as 'outliers' in the spectrum of human achievement, we regularly furnish these performers with a special type of social and aspirational status. They are often presented as targets for youth to model themselves on. In the 1990s, Gatorade produced one of the most popular television commercials of all time, focusing on Michael Jordan, that urged people to "Be Like Mike"

But, is this status warranted? Should we all aspire to be experts? If we understood the price these athletes pay for the possibility of attaining success – that's if they are lucky enough for everything to go right on the day when it matters – would anyone want to be an elite athlete?

Discussions about the development of exceptional sporting achievement rarely mention the costs of such devotion. The most obvious of these are the 'hard' costs like the financial investments needed to become an elite athlete. A 2015 Bloomberg article, for example, noted the British Lawn Tennis Association estimated costs of £250,000 ($345,000US) to develop a player from age 5 to 18.[153] According to a 2010 estimate of annual expenses of 'highly competitive' professional tennis players, athletes spent $143,000US each year, largely on coaching and travel, just to be able to fully participate on the professional tour.

In *Selling the Dream*, Campbell and Parcels describe the financial costs of participation in ice-hockey. In one section, they highlight six developing male hockey players in the 2010-2011 season who played at different developmental levels (i.e., minor atom (U9) to midget (U17)). During this season, financial costs for hockey-related expenses (registration and league fees, equipment and travel costs, as well as costs for any private instruction) for this single season ranged from $5,600 to $19,900.[154] Perhaps most notable was the list of expenses totalling over $8,000 for a 9-year-old player. Interestingly, none of these players seems to have advanced past the junior or university level of competition.

Less considered are the 'soft' costs like the loss of opportunities to do normal things children and adolescents do during development such as socializing with friends, video gaming, sleeping in, and eating fast food. An athlete who devotes 10,000 hours training for their sport (that tired trope again!) spends nearly 2 years of their waking life in practice.[155] When we add in the other elements of the high-performance sport lifestyle (focused time spent doing recovery activities, off court/field fitness training, team meetings, mental skills training and so on) this number expands considerably. One study from our research group explored the training histories of several hundred Canadian and Australian high-performance athletes from a range of sports, noting that one athlete reported nearly 22,000 hours of overall exposure to their sport (including group and individual practice sessions, mental and physical conditioning sessions and unstructured play-based activity) before the age of 18. This equates to 4.3 years of their waking life (~24%) up to this point, spent in sport-training related activities.[156]

There are also post-career costs. These can be relatively short term, as found in the 16% of NFL players who go bankrupt within 12 years of their career's end[157], or they can be longer-term, as seen in bodies that carry the enduring scars of the demands of elite competition. A recent study of British ex-Olympic athletes found 56% had experienced a significant injury during their career (i.e., an injury that caused pain on most days, that lasted for at least 1 month, and was diagnosed/treated by a medical professional).[158] As alarming as this rate is, these values are from athletes who survived the system and the rates of injury for those leaving the system are likely higher, maybe even considerably higher.

One of the most comprehensive research programs of long-term health in ex-elite athletes has been ongoing in Finland since the 1990s. These studies have generally focused on aspects of long-term health and chronic disease between athletes from different categories of sports (i.e., endurance, power and mixed), and compare these to profiles from the general population. In one study, they compared mortality effects in 900 male ex-elite athletes to determine whether participation in high levels of sport resulted in extended lifespans.[159] Ex-elite athletes were compared to their non-elite brothers, to help capture nuances of the early developmental environment, shared familial genetic effects and so on. As a whole, athletes lived longer than their brothers, but this effect was largely driven by the endurance athlete group; no beneficial effects were found for power sports. Intriguingly, the life extension in the endurance athlete group was around two and a half years (median age at death was 79.9 years for the endurance athletes and 77.5 for their brothers), which is eerily similar to the amount of time needed to accumulate 10,000 hours of training (~2 years).

Discussions of the costs of high-performance sport do not need to be perceived as attacks on this pursuit. There are clear benefits to the high-performance lifestyle, that go beyond the obvious ones like fame and achievement. In addition to living longer in general, high-performance athletes have lower rates of most chronic diseases then the average person.[160] But, it's important to know the costs associated with these benefits – costs that are rarely considered by the average person who just sees the flag being raised or the smiles in the post-championship press interview.

These costs are not restricted to athletes and their support systems, since many societies support their high-performance systems through taxation and other forms of governmental support. Discussions of the costs of sport should also explore how governments use public funds to promote sport in its various forms. In 2013, UK Sport, arguably the world's leading agency for the identification and development of sporting talent, published the results of an extensive project evaluating the characteristics of athletes who were 'super champions' (i.e., winning multiple Olympic and/or World Championship medals), noting that among several qualities that distinguished those at the highest levels of sporting success was a greater capacity to be 'ruthless' and 'selfish'. While these results need to be replicated in other countries and sports, as well as among more contemporary samples, they provide the basis for a discussion of what we value in sport participation. Is this something we should aspire to, regardless of the money or fame that may go along with it?

In order to conduct a thorough cost/benefit analysis, we need to have comprehensive knowledge of each element of the equation. This understanding is necessary so that athletes and their custodians can make well-informed, evidence-based and socially responsible decisions. While sport stakeholders have placed considerable attention to the processes of, and obstacles to, skill development, other elements have been largely ignored.

Models of athlete development, for example, focus on the early stages of skill acquisition, with very little exploration of skill maintenance or decline.[161] Across development, elite athletes usually see a gradual decrease in the amount of flexibility and control they have in how they organize their life, to the point that when their career peaks (in their 20s or 30s on average), almost every element of their lifestyle is designed to maximize performance in their sport. Consider this quote from Hall of Fame pitcher Tom Seaver:

> Pitching… determines what I eat, when I go to bed, what I do when I'm awake. It determines how I spend my life when I'm not pitching. If it means I have to come to Florida and can't get tanned because I might get a burn that would keep me from throwing for a few days, then I never go shirtless in the sun… If it means I have to remind myself to pet dogs with my left hand, then I do that, too. If it means in the winter I eat cottage cheese instead of chocolate chip cookies

> in order to keep my weight down, then I eat cottage cheese.[162]

Few of us are capable of understanding the level of dedication necessary for this type of lifestyle. In terms of human development, this way of structuring a life is atypical and we know very little about why someone would choose this existence, what the consequences of this lifestyle are on long-term development and well-being, or how we can best improve the situation. The average person has a life trajectory where they are just beginning to find their groove during the phase of life where the elite performer is reaching his or her peak performances. Moreover, the average person has a 30-40-year working life that culminates in retirement, and while this might not necessarily be the optimal strategy for a happy life, it's certainly one society better understands and has built appropriate supports for (e.g., career coaches, retirement programs). We know very little about how to support an ex-elite athlete who's peaked in the first third of his/her lifespan with the rest of their life uncertain. After a period of superhuman highs, how do we best manage the decline?

Leading National Sport Organizations are working to better understand how to support high-performance athletes post career. The past decade has seen a broad shift to issues of athlete mental health while in the athlete development program (e.g., as seen by organizations such as the Canadian Centre for Mental Health and Sport[163]) and proactive organizations such as the Australian Institute of Sport have developed programs to prepare athletes for life after their athletic career.

While there is growing attention to these issues at the highest levels of sport, there has been negligible interest in understanding these issues at other levels of the system. For instance, although the process of athlete selection is occurring earlier in organized sport than ever before, our understanding of the long-term impacts of these decisions on athletes is virtually unknown. However, it is reasonable to suggest that, at least in the short term, the consequences are serious since they have the potential to interfere with social relationships, affect individual beliefs in personal competency and undermine interest in long-term engagement.

Coupled with this is the belief among many sport stakeholders that any form of participation that isn't at the highest level has less value. Herein lies one of the great paradoxes of sport engagement. Sport has a special social power that can bring people together, break down barriers, and create icons. At its highest level, it shows us the absolute limits of our species. But, it can also destroy lives, leave families destitute and reinforce cultural and ethnic stereotypes. Done poorly, sport becomes a context for aggression and violence, rewarding characteristics that would lead to criminal charges and jail time in other settings. There is a dark underside to sport that needs to be part of the conversation about whether this is something we should advocate for our children, not to mention our time and tax dollars.

Eminence on the sporting field is an important indicator of the end point on a continuum of skill development. However, by placing a value judgement on one end of the continuum (that becoming an expert is aspirational with high social value), we also say something about those at the other end. The preceding chapters made the case that access to the types of resources necessary for athletes to develop and maximize their talent are not evenly distributed across strata of society. To a certain extent, an athlete demonstrating excellence on the sporting pitch reflects the biological, social, and situational advantages they've been able to experience across their development. This isn't to say personal agency and effort are not critical factors; they are… but it's much easier to persist in a demanding activity when key obstacles are moved out of your way.

We should also entertain the idea that the high-performance lifestyle with all its costs and sacrifices, is not for everyone. That said, there are certain types of individuals who might be perfectly suited to this type of life. Not everyone wants their entire life to be regimented and structured but for those who do, elite high-performance sport is a great fit.

Getting people to re-consider their own probability of becoming an expert in a given area will be a tough sell. In North America, and the United States in particular, de-constructing the national myth that anyone can grow up to be president requires a thoughtful re-evaluation of society's social structure. Meritocracies, as systems of competition (i.e., in sport as well as in society more generally), are only effective if built on participants having equal likelihood of success.

Chapter 11. Buyer's Remorse

On February 8, 1936 at the Ritz-Carlton Hotel in Philadelphia, professional sports in North America changed forever. The Philadelphia Eagles chose Jay Berwanger as the first player ever chosen in a 'draft'. The year prior, Berwanger was the recipient of New York's Downtown Athletic Club trophy for "the most valuable college football player east of the Mississippi". The following year, the award would be re-named The Heisman Memorial Trophy after legendary coach John Heisman. As a recipient of the award, big things were expected of Berwanger, who was known as a 'one-man football team'. These expectations… did not pan out. Berwanger is one of only two first round draft picks in NFL history to never play a single moment in the league. In Berwanger's case, the Eagles couldn't meet his salary demands so he took a job at a rubber factory and as a part-time coach at the University of Chicago.

In 1947, Clifton McNeely was the first overall choice in the first NBA draft. He was chosen by the Pittsburgh Ironmen, who were given the first overall draft selection after what is considered the worst season in NBA history. Like Berwanger, McNeely never played a single minute in the NBA and the Ironmen folded before the start of the 1947-48 season.

Not all first selections were this problematic. Major League Baseball chose Rick Monday as the first player in their inaugural draft in 1965. Monday would go on to play 19 seasons in the league with the Oakland Athletics, Chicago Cubs and LA Dodgers. Older Canadian baseball fans likely remember Monday as the person who hit a 2-run home run in the ninth inning of Game 5 of the 1981 National League Championship Series to sink the only real playoff run the Montreal Expos ever had. Long-time fans of the team still refer to Game 5 as 'Blue Monday'.

In 1963, the Montreal Canadiens selected Garry Monahan as the first overall pick in the inaugural National Hockey League draft. Monahan also had a long career in the league, moving from the Canadians to the Detroit Red Wings, Los Angeles Kings, Toronto Maple Leafs and Vancouver

Canucks, before ending his career back in Toronto after 12 seasons in the league.

These examples highlight the continuum of outcomes coming from draft selection. Sometimes things work out wonderfully, as with Gerry Monahan and Rick Monday, but sometimes you choose a Jay Berwanger or a Clifton McNeely. Given the amount of attention potential players get and the funds spent on scouting, testing and recruitment, why do some selections end up so badly?

The 'Tyranny of Talent' is not just found at youth and adolescent levels. It has important and obvious impacts on those at elite levels as well. We see examples of this in how professional teams evaluate players being considered for these leagues. Often the approaches used for assessing athletes at the highest echelons of achievement trickle down to policies and processes used by those working at other levels. We assume the qualities that are important for adult performance have equal meaning at lower levels of development.

Understanding how things are done at the professional level is useful for understanding athlete identification and selection more broadly for two reasons. First, identification and selection at this level occur relatively late in development (sometimes in high school but more often during college). As a result, the influence of random effects (e.g., chance, serendipity) and non-random effects (Matthew Effects) that occur across development are reduced since the prediction timeframe is considerably shorter. As a result, predicting performance outcomes a few years in the future should be easier and more accurate than predicting these in youth. Second, professional teams put enormous resources into evaluation and identification, which provides hard-to-get information about how useful increased attention might be for improving identification and selection. Put more simply, if accurate athlete assessment is a problem that can be solved by more money and attention, professional sport should provide us with evidence of this.

The first NFL 'draft' in 1936 was simply referred to as the 'selection of players'. Unlike the ages-old process for conscripting men into military service, which focuses on selection from the general population, the goal of the NFL draft when initially envisioned by Philadelphia Eagles owner Bert Bell, was to prevent costly bidding wars for talented young athletes and ensure that no team could monopolize all the best young players. Typically, the process involves each team sequentially selecting players across the rounds of the draft. Teams are usually arranged in reverse order based on performance in the previous year with teams that did worse having earlier selections than teams that did better. In an effort to prevent teams who are unlikely to make the playoffs from losing intentionally, some leagues (the NHL and NBA) have instituted a draft lottery, which slightly modifies the order of selection. The order of draft selection implies players drafted earlier are seen as having greater potential and higher market values than players drafted later.

Although there is variation across sports, each year eligible athletes from junior teams, high schools, or colleges around the world are evaluated to determine their appropriateness to play for prospective teams. The creation of sports drafts fundamentally changed professional sport, with greater focus now placed on understanding a player's potential for success at the professional level due to the considerable economic risk inherent in the draft selection process. The first pick in the draft can sign an initial contract four times the amount of the last pick *in the same round.*[164]

Ten-years after the first NFL draft, and based on the new importance of making accurate draft selections to gain advantages over other teams, the first full time 'scout' emerged. Eddie Kotal was hired by the Los Angeles Rams in 1946 and was their lead scout for the next 20 years, establishing many of the behaviors that would define scouting for at least the next half century, including long trips across country to see hundreds of players a year, extensive research and preparation prior to the draft as well as the philosophy of taking the "best player available" rather than simply drafting to fill open positions. Driven by the Rams' success during this time, their approach caught on, with most NFL teams instituting scouting systems by the mid-1950s. The scout has become ubiquitous in modern professional sport; the assumption that the secrets to individual player's future success are waiting to be poked, prodded and measured is widespread.

In addition to the regular scout visits to potential draftees, the NFL, NBA and NHL have long-established, pre-draft 'combines' where budding players are put through a series of (largely) medical and physical tests, presumably to determine their fitness for the rigors of the professional level and to gain additional information about their generic physical performance. Perhaps seeing the value in these types of events (and/or in the marketing showcase they provide for the leagues), MLB added a combine event prior to their draft beginning in 2021.

Surprisingly, there has been relatively little exploration of the long-term accuracy of professional sports drafts and their ability to predict success.[165] A recent review from our research group found only 18 studies focusing on how well draft selections related to future success. Furthermore, generally only first-round selections were related to longer career lengths, greater money earned, or better future performance. After the first round, the variability in players was too great for any associations to be identified.[166] The fact that the first round picks were most related to success seems like a 'no brainer' but the relationship between draft selection and future success is complicated – mostly because players are not fully realized performers when they are drafted and any developmental advantages they get after being drafted (e.g., more games played, longer periods to develop) may be important for understanding why they may or may not succeed.

Over the past few decades, thanks in no small part to the work of economist Phillip Tetlock and psychologists Daniel Kahnemann and Gerd Gigerenzer,[167] there has been increasing attention to the psychology of selection and prediction. Their research suggests an abundance of cognitive quirks and biases affecting how we make decisions. The sunk cost fallacy, for instance, refers to the tendency for individuals to consider how much they have already invested in a situation when considering future actions, and to use the amount already invested as a justification of further expenditures. For example, when you continue to sit through a movie despite it being awful, you are likely making the decision due to a sunk cost (e.g., I've sat through an hour already, I might as well see this through). In player selection and development scenarios in elite sport, sunk costs can be found when a coach continues to play an athlete in the absence of a performance-related reason to do so (e.g., when a star, first-round selection gets more playing time than a later selection who is playing as well or better). These effects were first shown in the NBA by researchers Barry M. Staw and Ha Hoang, who noted that players taken early in the draft played more minutes, had longer careers and were less likely to be traded than players from later selections, despite being equivalent in on-court performance. Similar effects have been found in MLB, the NFL, and the NHL.[168]

Another complication for understanding the psychology of draft selection involves the complexity of the skills and capabilities needed to excel on a professional sports team. As the old sports adage says, 'a good team is more than the sum of its parts'. Despite the tendency for coaches and scouts to consider potential draftees as separate and distinct entities, they must work as part of a team, where group interactions ultimately dictate success and failure. Good coaches know this, which makes it important but not any easier to accurately measure.

Consider the following quote about NFL coaching great, Jimmy Johnson, regarding his first-round draft pick (round 1, pick 1) of Russell Maryland to the Dallas Cowboys in 1991.

> To this day, Jimmy Johnson will insist that Maryland was the best pick he ever made as a coach. It's hard to figure by the basic way we judge defensive players. Maryland was never a big sack guy (24.5 for his career) or a big tackle guy. He made one Pro Bowl. He did not make an appreciable number of big plays that anyone seems to remember. But what Johnson believes is that Maryland was so solid, so versatile and so willing, that he was the guy who made the Cowboys defense go. He was the one doing all the bits of dirty work inside so that other guys could be stars.[169]

Consider for a moment the complexity of how Jimmy Johnson is rationalizing his player choice. The key characteristics – being 'solid', 'versatile' and 'willing' – are momentously difficult to conceptualize and measure (e.g., what does 'willing' mean? Willing to do what?).

Assessing and measuring these elements are challenging. The table on the next page presents the tests used in the draft combines for the major North American sports. As you can see, they are heavily focused on the evaluation of physical elements of play. This is no surprise; these types of qualities can be easily and objectively measured. How quickly someone runs 40 yards is also readily interpretable and, without a doubt, provides some indicator of physical prowess. Less often considered are other elements of performance, such as evaluations of technical or tactical skills. If these are considered at all, they are normally measured using some type of generic test that may not capture the nuances of the context.

Case in point, quarterbacks being considered for the NFL are typically required to take 'the Wonderlic'. The Wonderlic is, essentially, a test of cognitive capabilities – a form of intelligence test. In 12 minutes, test-takers are required to answer as many of the 50 questions as possible. The average score on the test is 20. On the face of it, the test has reasonable empirical depth behind it. It has been around since the 1930s and has a long history of being used in personnel recruitment and evaluation. It's been used in the NFL since the 1970s. Compared to other tests of general intelligence, it is shorter, but arguably equally valid and reliable, at least as a test of overall intellectual functioning.

	NFL	NHL	NBA	MLB
Physical Assessments	• 40-yard dash • Bench press (225 lb reps) • Vertical jump • Broad jump • 20-yard shuttle • 3 cone drill • 60-yard shuttle • Position-specific drills • Physical measurements • The Cybex test	• Bench press (50% of body weight x 3 reps) • Grip Strength • Vertical jump • Long jump • Pull ups • Agility • Balance • Wingate • VO2max • Push-ups • Upper body push-pull • Seated medicine ball throw • Flexibility • Physical measurements	• Bench press (185 lb reps) • Vertical jump • ½ court sprints • Lane agility • Physical measurements	• Physical Measurements • Posture • FMS • Vertical jump • Broad jump • 30-yard dash • Batting practice • Infield/outfield drills • Bullpen practice
Psych/Cognitive Assessments	• Wonderlic test • Interview	• Interview • Psych (personality, cognitive functioning)		•
Health/Medical Assessment	• Injury evaluation • Drug screen	• Medical exam • Functional movement screen	• Medical exam	• Medical exam
Multi-focus			• Scrimmages/Games	• Interviews • Showcase tournament (high school players only)

The ability of the Wonderlic to predict NFL success is a different story, however. A 2009 study found scores of the test among players in the NFL drafts between 2002 and 2004 were unrelated to future performance, selection position in the draft or number of games started. A more recent examination with a larger sample (draft classes between 2002 and 2012) found some value in predicting future NFL performance in quarterbacks. All this to say, results on the value of the Wonderlic test are mixed at best.[170]

The discrepancy between studies, and indeed the perceived value of the Wonderlic for choosing players in the NFL likely relates to its validity - the extent to which the test measures elements that are important for predicting performance in NFL players. Some variables, like general intelligence, would seem to make sense as being important predictors of performance in a dynamic, pressure-filled environment like the NFL, but it turns out, these variables don't have the predictive value one might expect. For example, do we really need NFL players to be intelligent in a general way? If they are 'football smart' then a lack of general intelligence may not matter. For instance, consider defensive end, Mike Mamula, who was chosen 7th overall by the Philadelphia Eagles in the 1995 draft, presumably, at least in part, because of his near perfect Wonderlic score (49/50).[171] Mamula, while playing a respectable 5 years in Philadelphia, eventually became a cautionary tale about reading too much into players' performance during the combine. In order to be able to pick Mamula in the 7th position, the Eagles traded their 12th overall pick and two 2nd round selections to the Tampa Bay Buccaneers. With these trades, and some other behind the scenes maneuvering, the Buccaneers were able to secure eventual Hall of Fame players Warren Sapp and Derrick Brooks, both of whom were available in the same draft class as Mamula.

The reason for this lack of predictability is likely one of 'representativeness' – the test doesn't accurately reflect (i.e., 'represent') the cognitive skills and capacities successful NFL players have that distinguish them from their lesser skilled, and less successful counterparts. There is surprisingly little research exploring the cognitive and perceptual capabilities of NFL players[172], but if the sport is anything like other forms of 'football' (e.g., soccer or rugby union), these capacities are important. In particular, better quarterbacks almost certainly have better decision-making and perceptual skills than lesser-skilled quarterbacks that allow them to make decisions more quickly and more accurately. These capacities are not captured in tests like the Wonderlic. In fact, some of the limited research done on the Wonderlic test highlights that it is a reasonable test of 'crystalized intelligence' (i.e., knowledge, facts and skills acquired through one's life) but is limited as a measure of 'fluid intelligence' (i.e., the capacity to flexibly adapt to emerging and novel situations). Fluid intelligence, in particular, is related to things like rapid problem solving, speed of comprehension, and abstract reasoning, which more closely align with the types of situations one finds on the football field than does the capacity to understand what words mean or recall general information.

So, what does the Wonderlic measure? Recall of general information, word recognition and understanding, and so on. It may be a strong predictor of how much time one has spent in a classroom in traditional learning situations, but it's ability to measure the cognitive gymnastics required for successful performance in one of the most demanding sports on the planet is likely minimal. An obvious question concerns why the test has continued to be used across 5 decades and likely reflects the simple reality that "nature abhors a vacuum". In the absence of valid and reliable tests of important aspects of cognition, lesser quality tests proliferate.

To be fair, designing appropriate, representative tests for broad application in the NFL combine would be difficult for a number of reasons. First, the perceptual cognitive demands of each position likely vary, requiring the creation of position-specific tests. Second, performance in football continues to evolve over time and so do the perceptual cognitive demands. As a result, tests would have to be updated on a fairly regular basis as the key elements of perception and cognition change (e.g., speed of play, changes in tactics).

It is not fair to just pick on the NFL since this is a problem in all draft combines. There is strong evidence that these elements of perception and cognition (e.g., 'how' to look and 'what' to look for) are critical for understanding athlete development and performance, yet they remain infrequently integrated into high-performance testing and training. Amongst researchers, however, there has been extensive and sustained interest in how these capacities support elite performance.[173]

In addition to the lack of valid and representative tests in the draft, the philosophical approach to selection may be inefficient. As noted previously, very early on in the history of the draft, the 'golden rule' was established. One of the unique elements of the selection process in the draft is that the population of players is constantly being updated and the player a team aims to take could disappear right before their chance to choose. As a result, most teams follow a philosophy of *taking the best player still available.* From this position, players are simply commodities that can be interchanged into computations of cost versus benefit. On the surface, you can see the value of this approach, especially in the "Moneyball Era" that attempts to make the evaluation of a player more objective, removing, to the extent possible, any emotion from the decision. From this perspective, players are stable entities whose eventual worth can be readily described like red and black lines in a ledger.

Although this has been the guiding principle for draft selection for decades, it likely doesn't reflect the complexities of this process. For instance, it assumes a) that players do not continue to develop after they are drafted, b) their development can be reliably and validly predicted from pre-draft indicators, and/or c) that all environments are equally capable of developing players to the same extent. More likely, different teams have different capabilities for developing players and these need to be considered when evaluating what a specific player means to a specific team. These decisions are not simply financial, or at the very least are not just financial in the short term, since a player's ultimate value is influenced by how well a team can develop that player to their potential (whatever that may be). A greater understanding of the types of environments related to, and needed for, successful development, could help teams gain more over the long term (e.g., what type of players can develop best in my system so that they have greater value in the long-term?).

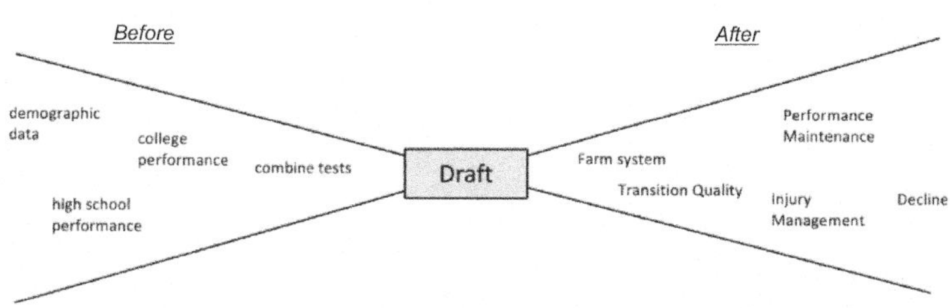

Elements with the potential to affect predictive accuracy of draft selection pre- and post-draft. Previous research has spent considerable time focusing on pre-draft indicators but comparatively less time on elements related to success after the draft.

Apart from a few progressive teams, there seems to be hesitancy in making these kinds of changes to how players are scouted and evaluated for the draft, which seems surprising given the relatively low validity of draft selections for predicting future career outcomes. Part of the explanation for this is undoubtedly the dominance of certain dogmatic approaches to 'how things are done' in professional sport. However, given the low accuracy of predictions in this field historically, the rationale for staying shackled to old ways of doing things seems weak indeed.

Section III: On Solutions - Simple Enough but no Simpler

A significant obstacle to improving the context of youth sport is that we have conceptualized an incredibly complex and dynamic outcome (human achievement and performance) using a very simple explanation. There is a quote often attributed to Einstein that models should be "as simple as possible but no simpler", which is a good approach to reducing what can often be complex discussions down to more easily understood elements.[174] *This section makes the case that, by clinging to the outdated nature versus nurture dichotomy, discussions of talent have been too simple. Our understanding of human development has advanced considerably since the mid-1800s (certainly it has since the turn of the millennium) and we shouldn't feel beholden to 'antique ignorances'*[175] *when formulating a 21st century approach to talent and its development.*

This section explores a more comprehensive definition for talent in sport (Chapter 12) that challenges the ways sport and high-performance athlete development have been delivered. Instead of focusing on talent as a fixed capacity, this perspective sees it as a variable that influences the process of athlete development. For instance, future champions must spend a large proportion of their waking hours either actively in training or balancing the recuperative steps necessary to maximize learning and adaptation. We know very little about the personal psychology involved with this type of mundane, repetitive existence, but it appears essential for the development of skills needed for future greatness (Chapter 13). Emphasizing the importance of athlete development as a process that can be nurtured and improved, instead of seeing it as an equation to be solved, challenges some of the foundational assumptions of current models and policies of athlete development (Chapter 14).

Chapter 12. Re-Defining Talent

At the dawn of the 19th century, two popular scientific movements sought to understand how aspects of an individual's physical appearance were connected to their behaviour and attainment. The first, physiognomy, was based on the notion that a person's character or behaviour could be determined by examining their physical appearance. Evidence of the popularity of this notion can be found in the character details of European authors from this time including Emerson, Poe, Dickens and Charlotte Bronte. The second movement, a more targeted approach than the first, focused on the size and shape of the skull as a reflection of an individual's strengths and weaknesses. Phrenology is based on the logical notion that the brain is made up of localized areas responsible for different functions (e.g., memory, attention, etc.). If the brain behaves like a muscle, areas that are highly active (either due to innate- or learning-related factors) will result in bulges in the skull in this area. Therefore, measuring an individual's strengths and weaknesses becomes a matter of determining the bumps and divots of their skull and understanding what areas these bumps and divots correspond to. For instance, the terms 'highbrow' and 'lowbrow' relate to elements of the forehead – those with a higher forehead (i.e., a high brow) were seen as being more intelligent than those with a lower forehead (i.e., a low brow). These movements are now almost entirely dismissed as pseudoscience and most laypeople and scientists look back with a dismissive 'how could we have ever believed that?'.

Up to this point, I've focused on describing what we know about sporting talent and the issues associated with the way talent systems are designed and delivered. There hasn't been much provided in the way of solutions. The fascinating thing about the evidence on each side of the nature/nurture debate is that both positions appear strong, and researchers are 'dug in' relative to their arguments. However, being able to argue for both sides of the debate means we've framed the research question incorrectly.

Because beliefs about talent and its development are entrenched in our social fabric, we are going to have to push through this concept to see what's on the other side. Part of this requires a re-framing, from the vague notions of talent used in coaching rooms and around watercoolers, to something that's more measurable, and, ultimately, testable. It's remarkable that despite the advancements we've seen in other areas of human development, our framing of the influences on attainment still usually comes down to this simple dichotomy of biology *or* environment, even in the face of mountains of evidence highlighting the limitations and inaccuracies of this approach.

Out-dated notions of talent are likely a driving force behind why youth sport is structured the way it is.[176] When we conceptualize talent as a generally fixed capacity needing to be 'identified' and then nurtured in an optimized environment to ensure the talent reaches its potential, we do a disservice to the complexity of this phenomenon. Similarly, blaming parents, coaches, and other elements of the system as 'the problem', underplays the complexity of how and why sport is currently experiencing these issues. It confuses effects with causes. The more critical question is not 'how do we fix parents who pressure their kids too much and too early' but rather 'why do parents think this is the appropriate path to success?'. Solutions need to be grounded in understanding the desires of parents and their expectations for their children. Although there are rampant examples of parents doing the 'wrong thing' in youth sport (e.g., shouting at officials or children during games), most parents believe they are doing something beneficial for their child's development.

Relatedly, we are quick to paint coaches as the 'villains' of athlete development when they put their athletes at risk for compromised mental health or physical injury, without acknowledging that most coaches believe these steps are required for optimal athlete development. To be sure, there are real villains in the landscape of athlete development and youth sport, but most coaches are compassionate and thoughtful in how they deal with their athletes.

There needs to be a shift from focusing on the problem as being related to behaviour to one driven by improper messaging or inadequate education. Given the preceding chapters outlining the causes of confusion in talent research, you could be forgiven for wanting to throw your hands in the air in frustration. Many have, some literally, but most figuratively, when they argue for positions grounded in 'talent doesn't matter' or 'differences between performers can be explained by practice'. But, acknowledging that talent is more complex than we thought doesn't mean it's unknowable… or at least more knowable. The limited information we have may provide useful clues for designing better approaches and environments for athlete development.

In 2019, Nick Wattie, Jörg Schorer, and I proposed a multi-faceted model of talent that incorporates what we've learned about human potential and development in other fields, but positions sport-related talent in this rather unique context. We felt the need to do this because although sport performance captures elements of other domains of human achievement, it ultimately extends beyond them. The physical and motor elements of athletic performance coupled with athletes' individual characteristics create a unique combination of biological, environmental, and developmental factors that aren't reflected in traditional talent models derived from cognitive psychology or education. As we noted in our paper:

> "Like chess, [sport performance] requires complex decision-making, pattern recognition and performance under pressure, but regularly requires the execution of these skills while an opponent is

> actively working to resist this execution. Like music, it requires the successful demonstration of highly complex motor skills, but also typically involves executing these movements while moving through an environment that is, to varying degrees, dynamic and unpredictable. Moreover, the perceptual-cognitive and complex motor skills seen in sport occur with performers actively engaged in sophisticated, and often fast-paced, deception to disrupt their opponents' performance."[177]

Our model highlighted a number of qualities of sport-related talent, the first, and most important, is that it is *innate*. Given the confusion about different terms used for discussing human development, performance and expertise, it's important to clarify precisely what we're talking about and how it differs from related concepts. If we don't center talent as reflecting innate tendencies, it is meaningless, indistinguishable from words such as skill, expertise, or proficiency. This point is important since there is variability in even how this element is defined. British psychologists Michael Howe, Jane Davidson, and John Sloboda, in their highly influential summary of innate talent, proposed talent as being situated firmly in genetically transmitted structures and therefore at least partly innate.[178]

Defining talent in this way makes it clear what we are talking about and differentiates it from Canadian psychologist Françoys Gagné's view of talent as "outstanding systematically developed skills" reflecting both genetically- and experience-based elements.[179] The concept of 'innate' is also complicated, but for our discussion, let's simply focus on it as reflecting qualities present at birth.[180] In our research and work with coaches, athletes, parents and other sport stakeholders, this is how most implicitly define the concept. It also reflects standard dictionary definitions of talent as "existing in, belonging to, or determined by factors present in an individual from birth" (Merriam-

Webster Dictionary) or "an innate quality or ability… that you were born with, not one you have learned" (Cambridge English Dictionary).

In addition to being innate, sporting talent is multi-dimensional, a conclusion that's obvious to any sports coach, fan or athlete. Exceptional athletic performance involves skills and capabilities in a range of areas (e.g., physical, technical, tactical, emotional, mental), all of which reflect degrees of learning and experience, as well as the impact of genetic factors on this learning and experience. This multi-dimensionality is important to note, however, for several reasons. First, research in this area has tended to take uni-dimensional and reductionist approaches to innate talent, likely because the concept is difficult to define and conceptualize. Indeed, the term 'talent' is implicitly singular, reflecting a single quality rather than the multiple elements underpinning an individual's performance at any point in development.

Positioning talent as a *multi-dimensional property present at birth* does not mean it's fixed or incapable of interacting with diverse environmental stimuli. In fact, an individual's sensitivity to how they respond to different environments (e.g., who is able to thrive in the high stress of a competition environment and who falls apart or leaves the sport?) is likely a key factor in understanding why athletes who may seem equal in potential early in development, end up at different end points.

One thing that makes forecasting and modeling athlete development difficult is that athletes can usually take multiple pathways and/or have multiple combinations of key variables to achieve elite performance. We tend to see talent as one thing, which is likely because of its link to notions of intelligence, but therein lies one of the problems. When we analogize talent in simple ways, similar to how we see more stable genetically-determined factors like eye or hair color, we imply it's easy to understand and identify, and that it is generally stable across development.

This doesn't capture the complexity at work and so we need to consider talent in a much more complex way. In the 1980s, psychologists exploring the interaction of genes across development argued that complex traits like intelligence and complex performance outcomes (e.g., sporting achievement) reflect intricate patterns of numerous genes working in concert (i.e., they are polygenic, as discussed in Chapter 6). Moreover, the interactions among these genes and the effects they produce are not simple additive relationships, but reflect processes that are multiplicative and 'emergenic'.[181]

Psychologist David Lykken and his colleagues proposed that most complex traits reflect combinations of genes, or partly genetic traits, that work through multiplicative interactions. Essentially, emergenic traits result from how an individual interacts with a larger system. Several variables associated with athletic performance appear to be emergenic such as creativity, leadership, personality, and recreational interests.[182] The relationship between genetic properties and height is a useful illustration of an emergenic property. As noted earlier, *hundreds* of genetic variants, in approximately 180 loci, constrain human height.[183] Adult height, which is important to performance in many sports, and is relatively straightforward to measure and forecast, results from a complex pattern of polygenic inheritance (i.e., DNA sequence variants at many genetic loci) and environmental interaction (e.g., quality of nutrition during early development). The full implication of the emergenic property becomes evident, and daunting, when we consider the multi-dimensional nature of talent and more complex traits than adult height.

In addition to this idea that genes work in concert through complicated, emergenic actions, their interaction across development is also dynamic. A simple view of genes is that their effects are expressed at birth and therefore easy to identify. This reflects the approach that youth who are exceptional at throwing, catching, running, and so on, at early stages of development must have the genes required for adult success. This view is certainly too simplistic to capture current understanding of genetic action. Genes are expressed across developmental time, which results in unpredictable patterns of development. This is especially true when dealing with complex outcomes like sports performance where the traits are polygenic and multi-dimensional.

These qualities start from an undifferentiated state and then move to different states over time. At the heart of a dynamic relationship is the notion that the process of development evolves due to subtle and not so subtle interactions between a person's genes and his environment. As neurobiologist Robert Sapolsky notes in his book 'Behave':

> Ask not what a gene does. Ask what it does in a particular environment and when expressed in a particular network of other genes…genes aren't about inevitability. Instead they're about context-dependent tendencies, propensities, potentials, and vulnerabilities.[184]

As if the conceptualization of talent as an innate, dynamic, multi-dimensional phenomenon that emerges across an unpredictable time course was not complex enough, complicated biological outcomes like elite sports performance reflect the effects of fortuitous gene expression. Many elements of development are random and unpredictable. As Keith Davids and I noted in our deconstruction of the nature versus nurture dichotomy[185], interactions at the molecular level have a degree of randomness in how biological processes such as transcription, protein synthesis and gene transmission are carried out. This means skill development will *always* have a degree of unpredictability.

The final element of a new definition of talent must recognize that development does not operate in a vacuum, and, as a result, the value of any given talent characteristic is determined by a host of other contextual factors such as cultural importance and relevance to elite sport performance at that specific point in time. For example, the cultural importance of bobsleigh in Germany is apparent (supported by a host of training facilities and human capital) and there is no reason to suppose that Germans are innately talented at "sliding down a manmade chute of ice in a small torpedo"[186]. In a different culture such athletes (e.g., those with superior genetic potential for power-based sports) might be sprinters, rugby players or American football players.

The anthropometric profiles of athletes from different sports have changed over time, altering the value of these variables for long-term development.[187] In sports like men's soccer and football for example, players have become taller and heavier as these characteristics have become more valued (e.g., associated with longer careers, better performance), suggesting a symbiotic relationship between the talent-related characteristics of the individual athlete, the value of those characteristics by the developmental environment in which they find themselves, and the task requirements of the sport.

A definition of talent as 'innate, emergenic and dynamic, manifested in specific areas whose value is determined by the context under examination' is a more accurate description of what talent means in sport, but it also adds layers of additional complexity to the process of understanding how it develops and whether it might be identified early. Further, these properties also don't really help with the problems of identification and selection since they emphasize the relationship between athletes' biological raw materials and its value in the varying developmental contexts the athlete finds themselves within.

Approaches to athlete development that select athletes early, coupled with the reality that these selections influence access to resources that are relevant for development, means long-term performance success will be compromised or inefficient. This is not an easy problem to fix, although generally there are two broad solutions. First, re-structure the world of youth sport so that these selections occur later (if they need to occur at all), or second, reduce the influence of these selections on long-term development. We explore the potential and application of these solutions in the next few chapters.

Chapter 13. The Mundanity Illusion

"At the age of 30, I quit my day job as a photographer to test the 10,000 Hour Rule – Dr K. Anders Ericsson's theory that it takes 10,000 hours of deliberate practice to become an over-achiever in any specific field. With almost no experience at all, I decided I'd try to become a professional golfer."
Dan McLaughlin[188]

In April 2010, 30-year-old commercial photographer Dan McLaughlin quit his job to devote his life to golf. His goal was to doggedly and single-mindedly focus all his energy to making it to the PGA tour. Despite the quote above, McLaughlin wasn't aware that Ericsson's notion of deliberate practice would end up justifying his whole endeavour, but he quickly became a devotee, tracking each hour of quality practice and training. 'The Dan Plan' – McLaughlin's website that contained details of each practice session along with his progress via an impressively declining scoring average – captured the interest of amateur golfers around the world who dreamt of their own personal 'what if' scenario ("what if I quit working in this 'hellhole' and just played golf every day?"), as well as skill acquisition and sport expertise researchers who watched a type of natural experiment play out that would be nearly impossible to replicate in a laboratory setting.

Ultimately, the Dan Plan ended poorly – at least as it relates to its goal of reaching the PGA tour. McLaughlin finished with a low single digit handicap, which places him in the 'good club player' category. This level of attainment is laudable, especially for someone beginning a skill acquisition journey at the age of 30, but it's also light-years away from the type of consistent excellence required for the PGA tour. The true value of the Dan Plan might be in emphasizing that the rhetoric around the development of excellence is not as simple as popular science books make it appear. Yes, practicing deliberately is important, but it's only one element in an amazingly complex equation. As an article in The Atlantic noted after the experiment ended:

"the Dan Plan crystallizes the sheer number of variables, beyond deliberate practice, involved in attaining excellence in a field—not least, reliable access to effective instruction and the support system and motivation provided by a cohort of peers striving toward the same goal. McLaughlin struggled to find both of those."[189]

Proponents of an 'everyone has talent' view of human development and accomplishment often emphasize the incredible devotion and persistence required for long-term skill development. Indeed, if focus of the debate were simply 'does an individual require large amounts of training in order to develop skill?' the answer is easy – yes! However, the confusion seems to be in mistaking the necessity of large amounts of training as evidence for dismissing a talent-based view.

In a highly influential article on '*The Mundanity of Excellence*' published in 1989, scholar and swim coach Daniel Chambliss de-emphasized the importance of talent as it relates to swimming performance.

> 'Talent' is perhaps the most pervasive lay explanation we have for athletic success. Great athletes, we seem to believe, are born with a special gift, almost a 'thing' inside of them, denied to the rest of us – perhaps physical, genetic, psychological or physiological. Some have 'it,' and some don't. Some are 'natural athletes,' and some aren't. While an athlete, we acknowledge, may require many years of training and dedication to develop and use that talent, it is always 'in there,' only waiting for an opportunity to come out.

In our research, most coaches and athletes see talent in this way – as a latent capacity waiting to emerge given the right environment pressures and supports, like a butterfly from its cocoon. While this conceptualization is an improvement over the simple nature versus nurture dichotomy, which proposes an either/or division between these influences, it still proposes talent as a relatively fixed entity simply requiring the appropriate environment to emerge. In Chambliss' article, which serves as an interesting precursor to the discussions about deliberate practice that would dominate discourse in the fields of education, motor learning, skill acquisition and athlete development a decade later, talent is dismissed as an explanation for athletic superiority largely because the life of the elite athlete is so mundane.

The subsequent three plus decades of research since Chambliss' article haven't done much to undermine this notion. The uninteresting truth is the high-performance athlete lifestyle *is* mundane, bordering on mind-numbingly repetitive to those on the outside looking in. However, this mundanity is not without purpose, and it hides important characteristics about human learning and achievement. Training effects work like compound interest for learning. They accumulate over time and there is a temporal 'sweet spot' between when the learning/training occurs, the brain and body's adaptation to the learning, and the loss of these effects. Furthermore, effects are not strictly additive in the sense that if you miss one training session you can simply add it to your adaptive response the next day. Effects are multiplied over time and while missing a single training session may not result in noticeable deficits, missing multiple sessions can retrograde performance and result in fewer opportunities for maximal adaptation. This was a key element of Ericsson's deliberate practice framework - that an individual who continues to put in high quality training on a more consistent basis will have a sustained advantage over her peers.

In the development of exceptional skill, this *Mundanity Illusion* reflects the tendency to see the mundane and normal, like waking up early to practice, orchestrating one's social schedule around training commitments, eating a healthy diet and going to bed early, as disconnected from how we think about talent.

Surely, the mysteries and complexities of talent can't be boiled down to something so boring? Realistically, however, the capacity to stay focused and committed to doing the mundane, ignoring social pressure, coming back day after day, is something many individuals would struggle with. Most crave variety in their experiences from one day to the next, and although the capacity for doing these types of mundane activities over and over again seems possible in principle, the reality is few would make the choice (either consciously or unconsciously) to embrace this type of lifestyle.

This attention to the mundane has not escaped the notice of researchers in this area. The past decade has seen an explosion of research focusing on understanding the psychology of practice behaviour. For instance, researchers have explored the potential value of various personality characteristics, not relative to how they affect performance, but as predictors of practice and lifestyle. The pattern of results reinforces this notion of 'sustained mundanity' as being critical for understanding long-term skill development. For instance, conscientiousness, one of the so called 'Big 5' personality traits, relates to the degree to which one controls aspects of their life in the service of their personal goals. Rating high in this personality trait is linked to superior performance and practice behaviors in athletes.[190] Related variables such as grit (one's passion and perseverance for long-term goals) and self-control (one's capacity to control or inhibit unwanted behaviors) are also linked to engagement in practice and athletic success.[191]

From the perspective of trying to understand this devotion to mundanity, emerging research takes on a new light. For instance, one of the most intriguing and controversial results from the Great British Medalists study was the supposed tendency for super-elite athletes (those who won multiple world championship or Olympic medals in their careers) to be distinguishable from elite athletes (international-level performers who never medaled) on feelings of selfishness and ruthlessness. For example, a coach of one super-elite athlete believed exceptional performers "have to be selfish, because you're so far off the scale in terms of normal human behaviour, that if you're not being selfish, then you are not doing your programme justice". The athlete the coach was talking about followed up with "You have to be self-absorbed and you know no-one else is really important; definitely I was the most important person in my world". The researchers saw these qualities as linked to super-elites' high 'need to succeed'.

There is a lot to unpack here, and the ultimate value of this finding is yet to be determined (for example, it needs to be replicated in other samples and more contemporary groups), but it is not readily apparent that these behaviors are really selfishness or ruthlessness in the more common negative sense these words have come to mean or simply reflections of the singlemindedness and clarity of purpose necessary for long-term devotion to a sport and all that entails. This distinction was noted by one of the athletes in the study - "I don't think selfish is the right word; selfish-driven, but yeah, a total focus and sacrifice all other things and all other people for yourself and for your ultimate gain."

Interestingly, work in sport psychology has not explored whether we can talk about positive elements like singlemindedness and focus without reference to qualities like selfishness. Furthermore, there may be implications to being selfish that involve negative short-term effects such as hurt feelings and compromised relationships, but positive long-term effects like better learning and skill acquisition. Athletes being selfish and ruthless in how they structure their lifestyle so they can optimize their training, would seem to involve a focus on the latter with the consequence being short-term sacrifices in areas of social and emotional health, in order to maximize the cumulative effects of sustained engagement.

If your personality makeup makes it easier to make these sacrifices, then this might be advantageous to long-term development. Not everyone is equally interested or invested in social and emotional elements of wellbeing. Some individuals can engage in training, especially persisting with the mundane elements, with less difficulty than others. That isn't to say those without these qualities are doomed to languish in mediocrity; it simply means they may need to take some extra steps to overcome these disadvantages.

Self-regulated learning, for example, is one of the current 'hot topics' in sport psychology and personal development. Originating in educational settings, it reflects processes related to an individual's capacity to proactively construct their environment in a way that maximizes their potential for achieving their goals, particularly as they relate to learning and attainment. The process of self-regulated learning is dynamic and cyclical, involving the interrelated processes of a) planning, b) monitoring and evaluating, and c) adapting. These processes affect effort and motivation towards specific behaviors like practicing, and they encourage athletes to think about their practice in unique ways (i.e., metacognitively).[192]

Early examinations of self-regulated learning and sporting achievement by Dutch researchers Tynke Toering, Marije Elferink-Gemser, Laura Jonker and their colleagues focused on these skills as relatively stable dispositions, that would apply across contexts. Their work showed good support for the conclusion that someone who has high self-regulatory skills in one area (e.g., sport) is more likely to be a high self-regulator in others (e.g., school). Reflection (i.e., appraisal of what has been learned and integrating this into future actions and expectations) appears to be especially meaningful for skill development.[193]

More recent work from our research group, led by my colleague Brad Young and his team at the University of Ottawa, has taken a different tact, focusing on how self-regulated learning capacities affect engagement in practice. Whereas much research in sport psychology has explored self-regulation with respect to explaining differences in performance, few studies have focused on how it can be used to understand and guide athletes in maximizing their engagement in training. Generally, the evidence shows strong differences between skill groups on elements of self-regulated learning for engagement in practice settings. More importantly, however, was the emphasis on self-regulation skills as being primarily relevant during periods of challenge and difficulty. This is not to say self-regulation is unimportant in a general way (i.e., more regulation is likely always helpful), but rather it stresses that differences between skill levels may come through better engagement in self-regulated learning when things are most difficult.

Establishing good self-regulated learning habits is critical for everyone but crucially so for future elite performers. As noted in the earlier chapter on 'labels', seeing your (or an athlete's) talent as a fixed capacity can be damaging to long-term motivation and persistence, arguably by undermining use of self-regulation strategies that help athletes maximize time in training. Perhaps the greatest contribution from Ericsson's work on deliberate practice was its emphasis on the *process* of skill development. Empowering athletes as active agents in their own development by using self-regulated learning strategies is critical for laying the motivational pathway necessary for athletic success. Maintaining these behaviors through the mundane lifestyle needed for long-term learning is part of the secret to greatness.

Chapter 14. The Accuracy/Striving Paradox

The 1997 film Gattaca describes a dystopian future world where humans can be genetically engineered to possess only the best possible genetic traits from their parents. This advanced understanding of genetics allows their society to determine who is best suited for various occupations – astronaut or scientist, cleaner or construction worker. Those who are genetically selected are known as 'valids' and gain access to better opportunities, occupations, and social standing, while those conceived naturally (the 'in-valids') make up the lowest levels of social class. The film's protagonist, Vincent, played by Ethan Hawke, is an in-valid who aspires to be an astronaut but this path is not open to him. Jerome, one of the other main characters in the film, is an ex-Olympic swimmer who shares his genetic information with Vincent, thereby allowing him access to the social apparatus that sees him appointed as a navigator for an upcoming mission to Saturn's moon, Titan.

The film is notable for its presentation of many of the key issues around human genetic engineering and the ethics of human modification, although not everyone was a fan. In his review of film for Nature Genetics, biologist Lee Silver notes that "Gattaca is a film that all geneticists should see if for no other reason than to understand the perception of our trade held by so many of the public-at-large" For our discussion, it provides a powerful 'what if' scenario that highlights several issues relevant to talent identification and athlete development.

My experience has been that most people who work with athletes believe one of two things. They either believe the process of athlete development is ultimately controllable through optimal training design and the management of environmental constraints or they view athlete performance as a 'Gattaca-like' formula where, although we might not be able to do it yet, eventually we'll be able to understand the variables determining athlete development to the point that we'll understand it with pinpoint precision. The former comes from a belief that we can manufacture an athlete's performance end points to be whatever we feel they need to be. They base this perspective on the near inexhaustible plasticity of humans in learning situations. The counter position, on the other hand, is grounded in a questionable understanding of research from neurobiology, neuroscience, and evolutionary psychology, where human behaviour is seen as a servant to the whims of hormones, genes and the remnants of our evolutionary history.

The battles between these perspectives are still being fought but the war has largely been decided. Much of the latter half of this book has been about shifting our perspective to recognize both sides are critical for understanding when athlete development works and when it doesn't. Our evolutionary imperatives, crafted in environments that look very different from the ones we operate in today and refined over millennia, are important. The role these evolutionary 'leftovers' play is sometimes large, sometimes subtle, but always there.

This complexity needs to trickle down quickly to how we conceptualize athlete development and operationalize what coaches, trainers, and other stakeholders do to promote this process. We need to move away from the notion that a single model can reflect the complexity of what's happening across development, and within a specific training environment at a specific point in time. The story of athlete development is one of variability, not stability and consistency.

Proponents of positive youth development in sport (a lofty goal to be sure), believe our focus should be on maintaining a supportive, caring environment where all can thrive. But this ignores the possibility that the environment best suited for one athlete's thriving (for example, if they are highly competitive, ego-driven and outcome focused) may be counter to the one that helps another thrive (if they are cooperative, low in desire for risk-taking and high in empathy).

Determining the 'right' environment for athlete development requires wrestling with key social questions. For instance, what is the primary social goal of sport? Is it to promote opportunities for a population to improve their health or to win Olympic medals to showcase social or political status? These are often put up as point and counterpoint but they are undoubtedly connected. When we consider indicators of health that are beneficially affected by a country's Olympic performance, we usually focus on physical activity participation[194] but those aren't the only indicators we could use to measure health in a population. For instance, suicide rates go down during important sporting events[195] but rates of domestic violence can increase.[196] Obviously, these relationships and the social and individual factors underpinning them are complicated, but they serve to highlight the complexity of the "sport is good for the health of society" message.

Similarly, what is the appropriate threshold for determining the success or value of high-performance sport? Many sports are supported through government funds, and, therefore, need to be open to discussions about whether these funds are being used wisely. For instance, if some of the seemingly negative results from studies of high-performance samples bear out under replication and extension, and robustly show a performance advantage to being 'selfish' and 'ruthless', how do we handle that information? What if, similar to other areas of achievement, evidence showed that more gold medals are won by athletes who score high on narcissism, psychopathy and Machiavellianism (the so-called Dark Triad of psychological traits)?[197] Since sport is socially supported in many countries, do we have a different obligation in regards to how we endorse or condone the activities and characteristics within this domain?

Finally, can we determine the right ratio of support for high-performance sport versus grassroots or participatory sport? In a resource-limited system, any government dollars that go into supporting high-performance initiatives are dollars that are not being spent on recreational programming. Although most acknowledge these two forms of participation are connected, our understanding of how they influence each other is surprisingly limited.

The Striving/Accuracy Paradox

From the perspectives of 'costs versus benefits' or 'likelihoods of success', we may not want everyone to think they can become the next Cristiano Ronaldo or Serena Williams. Not only does this devotion come at an incredible cost, as discussed in prior chapters, but that pathway leads to disappointment for the vast majority who attempt it.

The irony, however, is we still want large numbers of sport participants to strive for greatness… because we need them. In an opening chapter, I noted that the odds of a pre-high school player making it to the NBA is 1 in 70,000; but that doesn't mean the 69,999 other players have no value in a high-performance system. They underpin the system that develops the icon. For every sports superstar there are thousands of athletes and stakeholders in supporting roles, from the near-elite competitor who forces the superstar to continue to train and adapt, the weekend warriors and 'beer league' players who follow the superstar on social media, to the youth in the grassroots programs that form the life blood of local recreation facilities. All have a role to play, and the system is fragile to the point that removing any one element would have catastrophic effects on the whole system.

This need for competitors at similar levels of skill is important in other domains but never so much as in sport. Here, the capacity to challenge oneself against highly skilled peers is a necessity for skill acquisition and expertise development. Furthermore, this capacity for competition against highly-valued others is likely what draws many to sport over other domains of excellence.

From this perspective, we may not want talent identification and athlete selection to be much more accurate since increasing accuracy may result in more near-elites leaving the system when they are needed most. The Gattaca scenario, as interesting as it seems in a post-Genome mapping world, is unlikely because it ignores the psychological elements necessary for sustained engagement over the timeframes needed to acquire exceptional skill. Notably, the uncertainty involved in competing against similarly skilled competitors, without knowing who is more likely to succeed, is likely a key element driving commitment and effort. As a result, a critical issue for coaches and other stakeholders is the balance between having approaches to talent identification and selection that are reasonably accurate to allow the best management of system resources without being so accurate that they undermine the striving of those who may never achieve greatness but are so important for those who do.

This *striving/accuracy paradox* is not easy to resolve, and we may never get this balance right, but at its core, it emphasizes the value and contribution of every athlete in the system. Instead of being 'cannon fodder' in the high-performance system, non-elite competitors at all levels of competition are better positioned as the anvil against which champions are forged. Unfortunately, many athletes (and parents) tend to adopt an 'if it isn't elite, why bother' approach to sport engagement, which may undermine continued engagement for many young athletes. There is evidence of this in the declining rates of physical activity and sport participation in most industrialized nations, especially among children and youth, as lifestyles have gotten more sedentary.[198] Although there are likely multiple interacting elements explaining this decline, what is clear is that sport doesn't hold the same level of engagement, enjoyment or attraction to today's youth as it once did. The declines in rates of youth entering or remaining in the system have several repercussions. Fewer participants results in the creation of fewer teams in local sports leagues. This leads to leagues having greater variability in skill both within a team and between teams.

This disparity in skill may have important implications for promoting engagement and learning. Although we don't really understand the optimal environment for maximizing the learning process across all types of learning situations, we do know that if the task is too easy or too hard, we are unlikely to continue. In 2019, a study in Nature Communications proposed our optimal ratio of success to failure in simple tasks was around 85:15 – in other words, we'd like a success rate of 85%. This 'Goldilocks Zone' for learning reflects the psychological gymnastics our brain does when it ponders whether to keep trying at a task or move on to something else. This decision is becoming more and more important in a world where developing athletes have a vast range of activities competing for their limited time. Those with the highest level of early performance are likely fine because they'll receive positive feedback about their competency, which should feed forward into continued motivation; it is those whose potential doesn't emerge until later that would be expected to leave the system, likely to never return.

Once again, a subtle balance needs to occur between an emphasis on participation and personal mastery, which may be good for promoting retention and engagement in the majority of individuals, versus an emphasis on social/peer comparisons that may be important for the development of champions.[199] If we change the context of sport to focus only on participation, creating a celebration of mediocrity and sameness, we may erode the foundation of what makes sport such an important activity for human development.

Importantly, a key question for sport administrators and policy makers is 'what's more crucial for the system, accuracy or striving?'. This will depend on the priorities of the system; stakeholders in professional sports, for example are going to have priorities that are different from those working with amateur athletes. Similarly, the importance of selection accuracy versus personal striving will differ according to age and stage of athletic development. Striving may be particularly important early in development since skills and capabilities are still developing, and motivation and competency beliefs are still unstable. Unfortunately, this is where most deselection occurs, either explicitly, such as when a coach makes team 'cuts', or implicitly when young performers decide a sport is not for them because they perceive themselves as less capable than their peers.

Later in development, when motives are more stable and an athlete's identity is more strongly formed, personal striving may be less variable. Those who are homogeneous for the types of motivation, personality and other elements of psychological makeup best suited for the high-performance lifestyle, have already been selected to the system (or more likely, those without these qualities have been removed). At this point, selection accuracy may be more critical because the implications of selection are more severe. For instance, the significance of being deselected could be greater for an athlete with a robust personal identity as an elite performer. Consider developing near-elite athletes who have struggled for nearly a decade chasing their Olympic dreams only to be told by their coach that it's the end of their journey. The consequences of this act on athlete well-being are virtually unknown.

In many high-performance and professional systems, the struggle becomes balancing greater accuracy in athlete assessment and selection, without compromising the striving of athletes who are needed in the system but are unlikely to make it to the highest levels of attainment. Unquestionably, the most effective way to do this would be to limit the impact and power of selections on long-term development. This could be done in several ways, but it would require greater appreciation of the psychological dynamics occurring at different points along the athlete development journey.

During early periods of development, where young athletes may be more interested in fun and enjoyment, and have less autonomy in determining their participation (i.e., because parents are the primary decision-makers), coaches could interact with parents to ensure they understand the objectives and limitations of any programming decisions that might be interpreted as reflecting beliefs about talent. For example, coaches should emphasize the typically low accuracy of these selections and provide options to maintain the child's engagement with the sport. This could involve parallel development programs (e.g., other teams that train along with the travelling team such as seen in 'red shirts' or 'developmental squads') or providing more detailed instructions on areas to work on outside the program so the athlete comes back more capable the next year. Good coaches already do this.

Later in development, when athletes are more autonomous and the number of activities competing for their time increases, coaches might consider ensuring that at least some of the athlete's 'basic needs' are being met through their engagement. For instance, a coach might anticipate an athlete's competency beliefs are going to decrease due to being scored lower on a performance evaluation, but proactively works to ensure the athlete feels more strongly connected socially (increasing feelings of connection) and/or remains involved in the team's decision-making (increasing feelings of autonomy).

Ultimately, many coaches would move towards a more holistic and thoughtful approach to athlete development if they acknowledged how inaccurate their initial evaluations and selections of athletes are. The problem is many coaches approach this highly influential element of athlete development from a position of confidence, assuming they are highly skilled in assessing athlete potential. As noted in many 12-step recovery programs, the first step is admitting there is a problem.

Despite the financial hopes and dreams of genetic testing companies around the world, the likelihood of a Gattaca-like future for elite sport is highly unlikely for several reasons; here's two that might be most relevant. First, in addition to the enormous increase in understanding and measurement precision necessary to be able to predict even a single human's genetic destiny, this alone would not be enough for the simple reason that the outcome being predicted is not stable. Elite sport performance evolves over relative short periods of time as new technologies emerge, rules governing competition change and the upper levels of individual performance improve. Second, and more importantly, part of what makes sport such an interesting cultural pursuit is its unpredictability. It is likely that every increase in control over aspects of performance would lead to some related change to increase variability and 'noise' in the competitive system. Historically, we have seen some evidence of this; golf courses, for example, have gotten longer due to changing club and ball technology and sports like ice-hockey and baseball have modified their rule structure to increase the pace of the game. This focus on finding indicators of future talent and/or developing accurate predictive models of performance misses the point of sport. It would be hard to imagine what we would find interesting in some future state of competition where an individual's peak performance could be achieved with near 100% certainty.

Joe Baker

Chapter 15. Re-Creating Youth Sport

In 2013, the Rugby Football Union (RFU), the governing body for rugby union in England, held a symposium at the Royal Society in London. The focus of the symposium was on understanding the development of rugby union players. Amongst the many topics discussed at the meeting was the efficacy and value of the early selection decisions that were widespread in the sport at the time. After much discussion – largely focused on the lack of evidence to support this approach and the clear costs associated with these selections – the RFU made the courageous and risky decision to eliminate any selections for the National team program until the 'post-adolescence period'. This decision was courageous because despite the calls from researchers to restrict selections during childhood and early youth, elite sport was undergoing a movement to make selections at earlier and earlier timepoints in development. In taking this position, the RFU positioned themselves as leaders in incorporating the latest science on athlete development into policy. The decision was risky because many practitioners and scientists in the room, indeed most in the room, assumed that by being the only major sport to set this 'late selection' policy, the RFU would leave themselves open to other sports 'poaching' their best prospects before they ever emerged into the high-performance system. This didn't happen and by most accounts the policy has been a success.

Competitive and high-performance sport is in a period of significant change. Although the bulk of this change has been noted since the turn of the century, the seeds were planted early, through the evolution of broad social structures seen through changes in family dynamics, wealth distribution, and globalization. In the early 2000s, the pendulum of research and practice on athlete development swung to an apex where the focus was on high quality training, and lots of it. It's begun to swing back now towards a more holistic and nuanced view of athlete development where optimizing skill acquisition through appropriate training is just one of the factors we need to get right in order to understand how elite athletes get to the top.

Despite this swing back to a more representative middle ground, likely gone forever are the days when developing youth would spend most of their leisure time playing versions of their favorite sports in backyards and neighborhood greenspaces. We could spend our time lamenting the loss of this 'age of innocence' in the history of youth sport, which seems to be the tack many researchers have taken, or we could take what lessons we can and recreate the systems and environments for youth sport so that they better reflect the needs and desires of those currently in the system. The RFU's move to delay selection is recognition that the world of sport is changing and uncritically accepting established processes simply because 'that's how we've always done it' is ill advised in this dynamic environment.

Sport systems with limited resources will still need to make selections, but the approach to athlete selection will undoubtedly change, and rightly so. Sport stakeholders need to appreciate the ways in which youth in sport today differ from those in previous generations. The world of social media, virtual/augmented reality and multi-player online gaming have changed the social environment youth develop in. Even current elite athletes will have had a developmental trajectory with aspects that may seem alien to many young athletes developing today.

This emphasizes the problem of using models of what worked in the past as recipes for future success; they suffer from 'cohort effects' (i.e., variations in groups over time that affect relationships between variables). These changes have several ramifications. For instance, the attractiveness of other opportunities, an important predictor of commitment and persistence, has changed. How we determine the 'attractiveness' of different activities is highly nuanced, but generally it would be reflected in the personal and social pressures we feel for participation. For many, particularly during adolescence, social standing (e.g., what does your peer group value?) is a key motive for participation, and feelings of competence are usually interpreted through some type of social filter (e.g., what does this increased competence mean in my peer group?). Social pressures youth experience may give higher social value to spending time with friends online than to participating in sport, regardless of the level of athletic success achieved.

Approaches to athlete development have generally focused on creating models to help guide policy makers, coaches, and other stakeholders in managing athlete engagement. For instance, the FTEM (Foundation, Talent, Elite, Mastery) model for Australia or the LTAD (Long-Term Athlete Development) model for Canada focus on providing basic structures for the types and amounts of training athletes need at different stages of their development. This reflects the Standard Athlete Development (SAD) approach discussed at the beginning of the book. However, these models can be problematic because they assume similar pressures exist for different sports and genders, in different systems/cultures.

Recognition of the differing contextual factors affecting athlete development is critical since these factors underpin the most appropriate strategy for improving the potential for successful athlete development. However, regardless of the strategy, the following truism applies - *for athletes to continue to develop their skill, they need to stay involved.* In addition to the obvious and critical social implications of people turning away from sport as a primary venue for recreation, whenever athletes are lost to the sport or system, any resources that have been used for their development and any future potential they may have is usually gone forever. As a result, greater effort needs to be given to establishing patterns of participation first and foremost since all other elements depend on this.

Promoting persistence and commitment to sport training can be done in several ways, but generally these approaches fall on a continuum between two extremes. On one end is an approach focusing on mass participation in community sport and on the other is an approach focusing on smaller scale, individualized training for highly talented athletes. Quite simply, is it more effective to focus on quantity (lots of participants at lower levels of competition) or quality (supporting few participants with greater potential for success)? These two approaches are similar to two strategies explored in evolutionary biology in the 1960s for understanding species' continued survival and evolution.[200] The model, developed by E.O. Wilson and Robert MacArthur, proposed evolution resulted from either maximizing growth rate in a population (an 'r selection strategy', the 'r' refers to increasing the 'rate' of offspring) or by balancing growth rate with a population's capacity to nurture offspring so they had a greater potential to survive (a 'K selection strategy', the 'K' refers to *Kapazitätsgrenze*, German for carrying capacity). [201]

We can borrow this distinction and apply it to how governments and sport policy makers approach athlete development. An r selection approach emphasizes increasing the rate of athletes *entering the system*, such as when government funding is used to support grassroots and community sport programs. If we view athlete development through the participation pyramid (see below[202]), this strategy focuses on maximizing the base of the pyramid by emphasizing greater participation amongst the entire population.

In comparison, a K selection approach focuses on a smaller number of athletes, and improving the degree to which developmental environments nurture and facilitate their development. This approach emphasizes identifying talent early so it can be streamed into sport-specific environments that are rich in important training resources (e.g., better training facilities, superior coaching, highly-skilled peers).

Sport participation pyramid, modified from Gulbin et al. (2010).

To be fair, both strategies could be effective for athlete development, and the most appropriate and feasible approach depends on the contextual factors involved (e.g., what approach is more important to a country's culture?). Many countries use a combination of both strategies, at least in principle, but end up being constrained by government funding or changes in policy. Moreover, many of these contextual factors are already rigidly determined and would be difficult to alter without monumental social changes.

When sports have restrictive approaches to participation, such as early talent selection and competition streaming, it is easier for athletes to leave (or not join) their system, or at the very least, consider their options relative to other, potentially more attractive, activities. Recognizing the psychological processes occurring at this moment in an athlete's development should encourage the use of alternative strategies to maintain their involvement – especially given the poor accuracy of these early selections. For instance, clubs and coaches should consider ways to make it easier to stay involved such as removing barriers to participation, increasing the social value of engagement amongst the peer groups of interest, or changing the structure of the training environment to achieve the same learning outcomes in ways that are more attractive to this new generation of athletes.

An alternative to early selection and talent streaming would be to let more athletes stay in the system for longer. This does not mean keeping all athletes in the system, rather it reflects an approach that de-emphasizes the power of 'system-related selection' on athlete development. In this approach, athletes can maintain their involvement as they see fit. From a resource perspective, this would seem to require a greater degree of resources in the system, and this may be true initially. However, athletes who are not receiving the same degree of competence feedback compared to their peers or are not enjoying the increased training demands and competition stress will likely 'self deselect' from the system.

This may be a superior approach for a number of reasons. First, it removes the requirement for accuracy from the coach on whether this athlete 'has what it takes' to continue in the system. As a result, it's likely a more accurate evaluation of important success-dependent variables than can be evaluated by the coach. Second, it provides greater autonomy to the athlete and, as a result, likely affects the way they think about their sport experience as they develop - sport doesn't become a negative metric of self-evaluation, instead it may be seen as a domain of rich experience, but one where individual long-term success is limited. As individuals, we make these types of decisions about other domains all the time. We can enjoy the complexity of musical composition and song writing usually without the psychological baggage of our personal limitations being placed front and center. When we handle selection in this way, sport can continue to possess the joys of movement, energy expenditure, and challenge but without being 'that thing I tried but failed at'.

If we change the way we position talent and potential, seeing it as an evolving and emergent phenomenon, early talent selection is ill advised in most cases since the factors determining adult performance are not evident in youth (i.e., they usually haven't had time to emerge yet). Relatedly, focusing a developing athletes' engagement to a single area during youth also does not make sense since there is no evidence to indicate they are best suited for one sport over another.

A philosophy of athlete development that seeks to limit any policy or practice that narrows choices during youth is all well and good, but we can't ignore the reality that many sports have resource limitations that require them to make selections (e.g., number of qualified coaches, spots on a team travelling to a more elite competition such as junior world championships). This reality is hard to reconcile with the considerable evidence indicating our understanding of a player's long-term potential can only really be clearly estimated *over the long term*. A twenty-first century model of talent development needs to capture the complexity of the interaction between stable and unstable factors in determining a person's potential, along with recognition that this potential may only be understood after significant investment in training and practice. Early selection may be possible only for those factors that remain relatively stable across development (e.g., possibly some elements of personality) and/or can be predicted with reasonable validity and reliability from early indicators (e.g., adult height). The extent to which performance is reflected in these stable indicators reflects the value of early identification.

Think like a meteorologist

Similar to how sports fans critique long-term sports predictions that didn't pan out, the general public loves to pick on weather forecasters, typically without considering the complexity of the outcomes they are trying to predict. Over the past few decades, weather prediction has changed from vague "possibility of rain tomorrow" to specific "60% chance of rain tomorrow between the hours of 9am and 1pm". The fact that most people focus on instances where meteorologists are 'wrong' is a great large-scale example of what's known as 'confirmation bias', the tendency to pay more attention to information that confirms your beliefs rather than information that runs counter to them. The reality is the improvements we've seen in meteorologists' capacity to predict weather patterns may be the most impressive example of the practical application of science over the past century. Those in the field of talent selection and development could take a lesson from what we've learned in this area.

For instance, like weather, we would be better off considering athlete development as a dynamic process where prediction models need to be continually updated and refined as new information emerges. This would be an improvement over many current systems that see potential as largely static, just waiting to be uncovered with the right set of metrics. For instance, athletes showing better power, speed, strength at early phases of development are less likely to be construed as having greater potential for success if these values regress to average levels later. As we discussed in an earlier chapter, relative age effects highlight the persistent problems associated with confusing early size and skill advantages with greater potential. However, we could anticipate these biases and build 'failsafe' mechanisms (i.e., design elements that anticipate a specific type of failure) to account for them. For instance, we could delay any selections based on performance until later in development when maturational differences between individuals in the same peer group are minimized. An alternative, drawn from work by Steve Cobley and his team at the University of Sydney, involves creating correction factors that could be applied to the performance times of athletes to standardize their scores relative to their age.[203] In principle, this approach would prevent coaches from making judgements on unstandardized performance, which is prone to relative age effects.

In addition to this notion of individual complexity (i.e., the weather in a specific area, on a specific day will be complex), weather models anticipate that these predictions will also change over time. As new information emerges (e.g., shifts in global climate due to climate change), meteorologists try to determine what this means for their prediction models. Similarly, athlete development doesn't happen in a vacuum, and broader, global factors may be important. Changes imposed by sport governing bodies (e.g., modifications to rules, variations to sport funding) can wreak havoc on the efficacy of approaches to athlete development that see the end point of development as stable.

While the weather forecasting analogy works well, it has limitations, not the least of which is the problem of what happens to athletes who are not selected. In weather forecasting, the context that is producing the data is consistent. Yes, the information coming in is dynamic and emergent but the way the data are evaluated remains consistent. In sport settings, this doesn't happen, because each athlete is their own developing system. In addition to the individual psychological changes noted above, athletes are usually treated quite differently once selection occurs. Those with talent are given better coaching against better competitors in superior training environments. The others are usually left in mediocre environments with very little consideration to any type of later re-evaluation *just in case the initial evaluations were wrong.*

What makes this situation even more challenging is that coaches are very rarely able to make simple 'yes/no' decisions about whether their athletes have the potential for success; due to the complicated nature of athletic talent and the lack of robust early predictors, most athletes fall somewhere in the 'maybe' category. Unfortunately, most coaches have limited resources such as court/ice/field space, instructional time, access to leading technology and science, which limits the opportunities for developing athletes. As a result, coaches have no choice but to make decisions about who is the lowest level of 'risk' for their program – risks to the program if they lose a player with the potential for greatness, but also risks associated with keeping a player who doesn't have high potential but ends up taking the spot of someone who does.

What would happen if we didn't chase markers of talent in young athletes and didn't make selections until later in their development? Could more sports adopt the RFU's approach, which deemphasizes the impact of these types of selections during early development? In addition to the type of large policy changes made by the RFU, smaller changes can be done without much disruption to the overall organization. For instance, most coaches or sport administrators do not receive explicit instruction on how to select, what to look for and why, or how to manage deselected athletes. Recently, several leading organizations (e.g., the Football Association in the UK, the Australian Institute of Sport) have begun to increase the continuing education opportunities for these stakeholders so that they reflect 'state of the science' in how they manage and develop their athletes. However, this only improves the delivery of services to those who remain in the system.

Given the limitations in how athletes are selected and managed by high-performance sport systems, it would also be important to improve how we manage athletes who have been deselected, so that we increase their potential to re-enter the system later. For instance, given the evidence for low accuracy in athlete selections, coaches would be well served by re-framing how they discuss the selection versus deselection decision for athletes. Instead of presenting the selections from an 'all or none' dichotomy (i.e., "these athletes have 'it' and these do not"), coaches could be more forthcoming in how their selections were made (e.g., 'based on these metrics, the following athletes were selected'), as well as more cautious in what their selections mean for long-term-development.[204]

From this perspective, the coach's job doesn't stop at deselecting the athlete from their team. If anything, progressive and thoughtful coaches may choose to become more engaged, by developing approaches to help athletes with current gaps in their performance, for example, or by motivating their deselected athletes to keep training in the hope they come back stronger next year. Coaches and sport systems may also choose to invest in parallel development structures to explicitly focus on those who were near the selection cut-off and/or those who were missing qualities that are highly trainable. The use of 'development squads' and 'red shirts' are common in many sports, but could play important roles in youth sport to re-position or de-emphasize what a selection decision means.

Unquestionably, designing better youth sport systems will require a more comprehensive understanding of human development. Education has struggled with the issue of engaging young learners for centuries. Many of the issues dividing the field today (e.g., the value of specialized versus multisport engagement in childhood and youth) may already be answered in other fields of psychology. For instance, the value of play in early child development is strongly supported in the fields of evolutionary and developmental psychology and may help us ask better questions about 'why' it might be helpful for athlete development.

The most important conclusion from over a century of research on the nature versus nurture debate is how adaptable we are. When placed in varying and diverse environments, humans demonstrate an amazing capacity to match the demands of these situations. While adaptability and malleability are the defining characteristics of our species, this capacity for variability can be both a curse and a blessing for those trying to model athlete development. A curse because it seems there are always counter-examples for every model, pathway and trajectory identified by researchers, which negatively affects uptake of these models into policy. A blessing because it reinforces the conclusion that these models do not have to be prescriptive or deterministic.

To be sure, approaches that focus on individual systems or specific athletes are limited in what they tell us about the generalities of athlete development because it is too easy to find cases to fit the narrative the author wants to tell. For instance, they may tell us that it's possible to create athletes if you provide enough resources for them, but this doesn't mean it's a good use of public funding. Sport systems with limited resources often need to be focused on issues of efficiency over effectiveness.

Let's imagine a different type of approach to developing athletes, where young athletes are not seen as 'hard wired' for a specific sport or activity. They don't come already pre-determined to excel as hockey players, quarterbacks or distance-runners. Instead, they are 'pre-wired' for success in certain 'areas' of engagement. A similar approach to this notion of pre-wiring was used in the development of the 'Sports Compass' by sport scientist Johan Pion.

This initiative was developed in Flanders, a small region in Belgium to try to improve the efficiency and effectiveness of athlete development programs. It involves a broader approach to determining the types of sports children and youth might be best suited for, based on personal interests, developing motor skills/competencies, and availability. In this multi-phased approach, children begin by describing what they 'like to do' and what they 'do well'. They are then presented with a list of potential sports and activities that fit with their interests and capabilities. The objective of this initiative was to marry the needs of high-performance programs (e.g., talent identification/selection and transfer) with individual athlete's needs to participate in activities they enjoy and feel competent performing. This approach emphasizes the value and potential when athlete development initiatives are grounded in the unique motives, wants and desires of the individual athlete.

Regardless of how and when they get there, elite athletes eventually find themselves in a highly focused athlete development environment. In an ideal situation, we'd be able to describe how an individual's genetic makeup interacts within different environments according to what are referred to as 'norms of reaction', a concept originating in 1909 by the German zoologist, Richard Woltereck. In simple contexts, identical organisms could be placed in different environments so that the range of responses could be detailed, such as in plant breeding. The goal here is to develop a continuum of possible reactions in the phenotype from the identical genotype to understand the roles of different environments.

You could imagine how useful this would be for designing the best environments for athletes to thrive. In sporting environments, however, this is not possible due to the complexity of the different types of environments *and* the genotypes of athletes therein. However, studies of 'discordant identical twins' provide some insight. For instance, a recent study of active versus inactive identical twins found the Achilles tendon in the active twin was stiffer than in the less active one, presumably due to their activity engagement.[205] If these differences in activity patterns emerge in later life (e.g., middle age), differences between active and inactive twins include higher endurance capacities, lower body fat percentages, better metabolic profiles (i.e., insulin function) and superior indicators of brain function in the twin who stayed active. [206] While these twins were nowhere near the level of training and skill as elite performers, the results suggest a diverse range of 'reactions' from general participation in sports and exercise.

While genetic factors have been implicated in exercisers' and athletes' perceptions of the benefits of, and barriers toward, involvement in sport and exercise[207] they haven't been explored using the same 'active twin vs non-active twin' designs used in studies of physical outcomes. Despite most of the discussion of norms of reaction focusing on physical outcomes, different environments will undoubtedly also influence feelings of motivation, competence, and other psychosocial predictors of long-term behavior and development.

From the perspective of general 'pre-wiring', early streaming is not necessary, at least in large numbers. Although those with greater access will be able to take advantage of opportunities they have that others don't (e.g., due to greater financial resources to pay for things like private instruction), a more effective general approach to youth engagement would be to provide greater access to as many sporting opportunities as possible during early development. This could be done by exposing a greater proportion of developing youth to a more expansive range of movement and sport experiences either through traditional physical education curricula or by reducing barriers to access and increasing availability of grassroots, participatory sport programming.

By making early streaming unnecessary, coaches can use a greater amount of their time to focus on designing environments for skill acquisition, providing better feedback, and focusing on satisfying the unique needs of learners in their sport. Providing a greater number of developmental opportunities for young athletes should increase the potential for those with 'talent' to find the right sport for this capacity to thrive. Moreover, it would keep more youth involved in sport for longer, particularly during impressionable stages of growth, maturation and development.

It's important to highlight that the validity and feasibility of these approaches are unclear. Although they appear to fit with existing research and understanding of human motivation and behavior, their ultimate value can only be determined through extensive, long-term assessment. However, it is also noteworthy that existing models have precisely the same problem. The SAD approach seems to have been created more out of logistical and administrative convenience rather than grounding in the sciences of human nature and development. As a result, there's no reason to feel beholden to current systems or approaches.

Chapter 16. No-Size-Fits-All

In the 1990s, a group of Canadian sport stakeholders created the Long-Term Athlete Development model, which became the first widely-used model of athlete development, first in Canada and then around the world. Similar models emerged in other countries, to the point that most sporting nations now have some form of standardized framework representing their process of athlete development.

In most high-performance settings, these frameworks are designed to allow administrators to allocate resources more efficiently, and for coaches to identify developmental priorities. From this perspective, they may seem to be useful approximations of the pathway from sport beginner to adult champion. However, at their core, they assume the pathway to success can be reduced to a single, simple trajectory.

In sport, as noted in previous chapters, the phenomenon most coaches (and scientists!) describe as 'talent' is not a single thing. It's the reflection of a collection of often disparate variables manifesting into displays of performance that have meaning at specific points in time and for each individual. From this viewpoint, the notion of talent identification and selection should more accurately be called 'talents identification/selection' (or elements of talent) since it's the unique combination of variables that results in a person's performance and development. A grounding of talent in innate factors, coupled with the 'first law of behavioral genetics' (i.e., all behavioral traits are heritable), means if there are 100 variables affecting an individual's performance at a given point in time, there are 100 elements of talent at play. To paraphrase Robert Sapolsky's quote from Chapter 12, each element needs to be considered relative to what it means in a particular environment and at a specific point in development.

Furthermore, these variables change across development; the elements of sporting success in youth look different than in adolescence because the requirements of performance are different. Early in the skill acquisition process, there is a greater reliance on simple execution of the motor skills necessary for the sport. Success is often determined by those athletes who can execute these skills most consistently. In addition, the factors that predict success differ across development for other reasons – the cohorts of athletes are changing. Height may be an important predictor of performance and success in sports like volleyball and basketball early in development, but its importance is reduced later in development, not because height is no longer important, but because the athlete cohorts have become homogeneous for height (i.e., all the players are tall). This element of talent has changed as the population has changed.

Similarly, the elements that constitute talent in one sport can be vastly different from other sports due to the uniqueness of the performance demands. This is one of the reasons talent is so difficult to capture and evaluate accurately. Athlete identification and selection in sports like rowing, for example, may be easier because the complexity of the sport is lower compared to sports like soccer and basketball. This complexity is reflected in the differences in performance environments (soccer and basketball take place in environments that are much more dynamic and unpredictable than rowing). It's also reflected in the depth of competition internationally, number of players on the team, intricacy of the rules and regulations and so on.

An athlete's performance, at any point in their development, is made up of a range of variables, each having the characteristics of talent identified above. In order to identify these variables, answers to several questions are needed:

- What are the key elements of performance at this stage of development (childhood, youth, adolescence)?
- How do these indicators relate to the type of performance we hope to see at the adult level?
- To what extent are these elements fixed versus malleable/unstable across the developmental pathway?

We also need to acknowledge that one of the issues that makes the process of athlete development so challenging is that it involves identifying the types of variables that are helpful for predicting the future (the identification/selection part) while also providing and maintaining the appropriate environments for continued interest and long-term engagement (the development part). In designing sport systems that emphasize identification and selection instead of interest and engagement, we put the 'cart before the horse'.

The influence of these elements of talent is seen in a range of areas across development – from the very first minute of an athlete's practice until the point they achieve their highest level of attainment, whatever that ends up being. For instance, some youth are more interested in sensational and risky activities and seek out these types of engagement, while others are more content with more muted pursuits. Even here the effect is not simple. It may be driven by desires or motives to feel these increased sensations (traditional sensation-seeking behaviour) and/or a muting of biological elements that result from the activity, thereby leaving them in a position for greater success (improved coping behaviors). Currently, the poster-boy for this combination of factors would appear to be free climber Alex Honnold, who reports a keen interest in extreme, highly sensational activities but whose amygdala (the brain's fear center) may not process stress the same way as an average individual.[208]

In a similar way, variables related to one's interest or persistence over time with an activity likely differs between individuals. These are reflected in differences between athletes in motivational capacities like work ethic, effort, and drive as well as in qualities that affect how an individual experiences events during their development such as resiliency, adaptability and forms of self-efficacy.

The extent to which these variables have value for predicting future success relies on a) their relative importance to adult-level performance and b) the degree to which this variable is changeable in different developmental environments. For example, height is a key performance-related characteristic in sports like basketball, volleyball and rowing, and adult height is highly predictable using sex-based maturity and height velocity curves. As a result, the extent to which height is relevant to a sport will directly affect how accurate athlete selections based on height will be. If early selections are based on height, and adult height is important for elite performance, selections will have a higher level of accuracy. It hardly bears stating, however, that even in sports where height is obviously critical, it is not the only relevant performance-related variable, and shorter players can succeed.

In order to have high levels of accuracy, all performance-related variables would need to have similarly accurate and precise early indicators, which is unlikely given the complexity of the variables involved. As a result, early talent selection is limited to the extent to which the elements being measured are stable over time. These relationships may reflect direct indicators of future potential (e.g., the aforementioned height but also some measures of personality at some points in development[209]) or indirect indicators (as simply reflecting those who are better performers at that time). Sports where elite performance is less determined by these types of stable factors will be less predictable (e.g., sports that take place in complex and dynamic environments where decision-making, anticipation and creativity are more critical for performance).

If one takes more than a superficial glance at most sports, it's clear they take place in environments that are more complex than can be predicted by these simple approaches to selection/identification. These approaches to athlete identification and selection are misplaced (at best) or destructive (at worst). Misplaced because they do not capture the complexity of the process they are trying to predict; destructive because they could promote selection of those who show signs of initial success but little long-term potential.[210]

Unfortunately, the juggernaut that is youth sport doesn't capture the nuances of human development, sport performance or the psychology of human decision-making very well. With few exceptions, government-funded sport systems do not try to capture the unique elements that might make early identification, selection, and streaming more appropriate for some sports compared to others. However, understanding the complexity of different contexts and environments is a good place to start the discussion. As noted, this complexity comes in many forms.

Performance complexity: Sports vary in the level of complexity performers face when executing the requirements of their sport. In motor learning, this distinction is often simplified as 'open' versus 'closed' environments, with open environments reflecting more dynamic contexts with rapidly changing inputs (e.g., soccer players) and closed environments being more stable and predictable (e.g., gymnasts executing a well-rehearsed tumbling run in a floor routine). Although this distinction has limits – no environment is completely 'closed' since crowds, environmental noise, and so on will always vary, and similarly many 'open' sports have elements of performance that are more 'closed' (e.g., the free throw in basketball or penalty kick in soccer) – it is useful for capturing the extremes in the dynamics of performance environments.

Developmental complexity: The developmental context an athlete finds themselves in can vary considerably and, coupled with individual developmental factors, results in a complex web of interactions among relevant variables. Individual developmental factors such as rates of growth or training experience mean different things in different contexts. A later-than-average start to sport-specific training, for instance, likely has less impact on an athlete's career potential in a sport like triathlon than it does in gymnastics. Similarly, the necessity of resources such as high-quality coaching, similarly skilled peers, and high levels of socioeconomic support varies by sport. In some contexts, these and other resources are prerequisites for early development, in others, they are simply stumbling blocks - obstacles to be overcome if other variables are favourably aligned.

Historical complexity: In addition to these more obvious forms of complexity, sports evolve over time, leading to greater sophistication and, almost without exception, greater difficulty. The trajectory sports follow as they morph and evolve due to cultural and social pressures are unpredictable, even in relatively 'simple' sports.[211] For instance, sports can experience rapid changes due to advancements in technology (e.g., Speedo's 'Fastskin' suit in swimming or Nike's Vapour Fly in running), changes in government funding (e.g., as when countries are awarded major events like Olympic Games), modifications of technique (e.g., the first use of the 'flop' technique by Dick Fosbury in high jump) or shifts in cultural importance (e.g., as seen in Kenyan running after the success of Kipchoge Keino in the 1960s).

There hasn't been much thought given to the role of between sport differences in these areas (not to mention differences that may occur 'within' a sport due to cultural/social influences, etc.), but they will have important implications for understanding talent identification and selection (e.g., is the developmental context too complex for accurate identification of long-term potential?), performance forecasting (e.g., how is the sport going to change in the next 10 years and does this athlete have the right profile to match this change?) and skill acquisition (e.g., given all we know about the positives and negatives of athlete development, what is the 'best' environment for this athlete at this stage of his or her career?).

In his recent summary of the nature and nurture of neurological and brain development, neuroscientist Kevin Mitchell argued there is very little influence of 'nurture' directly on an individual's development and behaviour. Instead, he argues people construct their own environment rather than the environment constructing them. This assumes people seek out existing environments based on their genetic predispositions and modify them to increase their likelihood for success (e.g., tall people will seek out environments where they are more likely to be successful such as basketball, not gymnastics). Sporting systems that stream athletes into competitive levels and make early choices about who is more likely to be successful, limit the capacity for athletes to seek out these opportunities. Once again, a more beneficial approach would be to provide as many chances as possible to developing youth, which would allow them to 'discover' the sport type and level of competition that best fits their unique set of developmental and personal constraints. Those with high neuroticism. for example, might seek a sport that satisfies those needs (e.g., elite, mainly individual sports) while those with high extraversion might seek out social, team-based activities. In many countries, the sport system fails because it creates an environment that limits and constrains what an individual is able to experience.

Of all the possible ways in which we could consider athlete development, we have the 'one size fits all' perspective at one extreme with an 'every pathway is random, nothing is predictable' at the other. As with most elements of human behavior and development, the most defendable approach likely lies somewhere in the middle. Athlete development may be messy, complicated and difficult to predict, but that doesn't mean the process of athlete development is the end result of some sort of 'random pattern generator', creating pathways anew for each athlete.

More likely, there are archetypes of athlete development that reflect clusters of psychological, physical and social variables relating to flexible, but predictable, pathways of development. We see evidence of these in some models of athlete development. The Developmental Model of Sport Participation developed by sport psychology researcher Jean Côté, for example, notes athletes can follow an early development pathway that reflects specialization in a single sport or an approach that involves 'sampling' from many sports.[212] This distinction emphasizes that the social and personal factors influencing how an athlete experiences sport and what they do in those experiences is more nuanced that can be captured in models with a single pathway.

That said, the subtleties of athlete development are almost certainly more complicated than this, as raised in recent concerns about the simplicity of the 'specialization' versus 'sampling' dichotomy.[213] However, that does not mean there is no value in considering 'archetypes' of athlete development.[214] For instance, the figure below provides a simple, hypothetical grid on which different athlete development archetypes could be placed.

The y-axis reflects the extent to which an athlete's current performance is believed to be the result of exceptional natural ability (i.e., the 'natural') or the result of hard work (i.e., the 'striver'). On the x-axis, an athlete can be seen as being a better candidate for an elite performance system due to comparisons to their peers based on physical/technical skill (i.e., the technically proficient player) or their cognitive/psychological characteristics (i.e., the good 'decision-maker' or the player with the 'killer instinct').

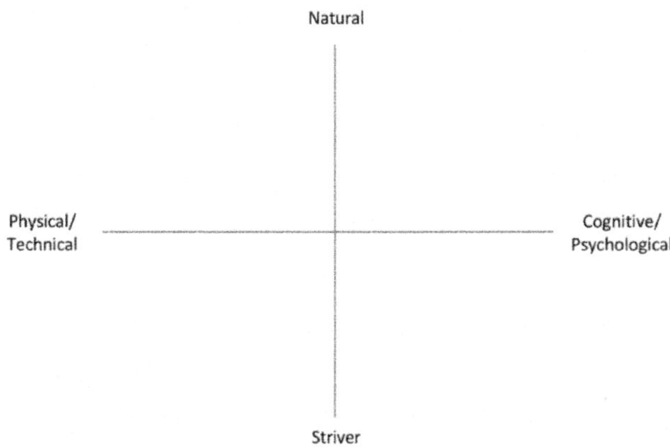

To be clear, these grid poles represent extremes of a very crude continuum, and there are undoubtedly combinations and interactions between these elements in explaining optimal athlete development and performance.

That said, the idea of archetypes provides a useful platform for discussing the limitations of current models of athlete development. The early emphasis on physical aspects of performance, as reflected in persistent biases like the relative age effect, likely increases the potential for archetypes related to physical/technical skill and/or natural ability to be selected into the system. The flipside of this is that strivers, who may have lower initial levels of skill but greater potential to develop over the long term, and those with higher potential in cognitive and psychological elements of eventual performance, are more likely to be removed from the system through deselection. As a result, those who eventually emerge at the end of the high-performance pathway may reflect a tendency towards early physical and technical skill. However, this is likely due to selection biases rather than the inherent value of these early capabilities. Early selection pressures will place disproportionate value on elements that distinguish those with stronger early performance, but this does not mean those elements are most important or valuable for later performance.

A 21st century approach to talent should involve greater focus on the process of athlete development and reflect a combinatorial relationship between genetic and environmental factors. This relationship will continue to be nearly impossible to dissect, except in simple sports or athletes with once-in-a-generation abilities. Moreover, we have to consider the role of luck and random chance, which can influence athlete development in ways subtle (being in the right place at the right time) and complicated (random genetic or biological noise). As noted by cognitive psychologist Steven Pinker in *How the Mind Works*, life does not have the inherent structure and understandability of chess, it is more like backgammon, with the roll of the dice on every turn.[215] At the end of the day, there is no basis for feelings of certainty in athlete development predictions.

No model can ever hope to capture all the intricacies and nuance of athlete development and the closer one looks at how to maximize one specific person's development, the less they will find the general model applies. A superior approach is to consider predictions about an athlete's potential for success as a type of likelihood estimate, with a degree of error and inaccuracy built into how these numbers should be considered. However, this type of probabilistic assessment is not 'natural' for our mind, which usually considers decisions as simple binaries, and usually with high confidence about our ability to predict the outcome. As a result, sports systems will need to ensure mechanisms are in place to make nuanced decision-making more likely to occur. While much of the focus in the area of 'decision-making hygiene' has focused on improving how data are collected and interpreted, in sport, this needs to start with a clear understanding of what an athlete's data mean and what it is being interpreted against. A more fruitful and evidence-informed approach to modeling athlete development (indeed, for any athlete interaction) would see athletes taking one of several possible trajectories they could follow to successfully navigate the high-performance system. The poor accuracy of most selection decisions means any credible model of athlete development needs to be flexible and anticipate obstacles that may impede an athlete's continued engagement in the system. Given the low rates of youth engagement in sports and physical activity, high-performance systems should be doing everything they can to maintain all athletes' engagement, at any level, for as long as possible.

Epilogue

Notions of talent will remain popular topics for self-help books claiming to know the answer to human achievement. Sound bites like 'talent doesn't matter and 'everyone can be a genius' are appealing; they're just not true. The reverse, that talent is a powerful and direct influence on your life and potential, is also not true except in extreme and/or very simple contexts. The answers to most problems to do with human behavior are more complicated than can be captured in a newspaper headline or TikTok video.

Understanding what to do with notions of talent, and how they relate to how we deliver youth sport, work with child and adolescent athletes, and evaluate future professional players, is equally complicated. In a 2020 episode of his Origins podcast with Joseph LeDoux, theoretical physicist Lawrence Krauss laments the problem of those working to understanding cognition, consciousness, and other elements of the brain. Despite an early interest in neuroscience, he notes he "took the easy route, which was to understand the universe", humorously emphasizing the complexity of the task facing those of us trying to understand the psychology of human performance.[216] Part of the solution for moving forward in a field which has been bogged down in simple models and explanations for over 150 years is recognizing this complexity, and embracing the difficulties in trying to explain it.

Importantly, we shouldn't want these simple explanations to be true. In the words of evolutionary biologist Theodosius Dobzhansky: "genetic diversity is mankind's most precious resource, not a regrettable deviation from an ideal state of monotonous sameness."[217] The diverse variation we see in our population drives evolutionary change. It has been the driving force in our species' evolution for approximately six million years and there's no evidence that this process is over. Less often acknowledged is the role this population variability plays in driving the creative and novel achievements we continue to see in all elements of our culture. Most sports would be uninteresting without this variation in how successful performance is produced.

Acknowledging this complexity allows for approaches to athlete development that are grounded in evidence rather than policy and rhetoric. For instance, what is the evidence to support early streaming of athletes into sports through talent identification exercises? Is an early environment rich in high quality coaching, the best training equipment and a highly skilled peer group really superior to less structured approaches with greater variability in training design as well as in the capabilities of opponents and teammates?

Renowned evolutionary biologist J.B.S. Haldane once wrote "my own suspicion is that the universe is not only queerer than we suppose, but queerer than we *can* suppose. I suspect that there are more things in heaven and earth than are dreamed of, or can be dreamed of, in any philosophy" and I suspect this is how we should consider the issue of talent. The prediction of long-term development in humans will, to an extent, always be unknowable. This is what makes us so interesting. For those working in most sports, particularly at early levels of development, where the efficient use of limited resources is a necessity, increasing the accuracy of the system by even a few percent would translate to important savings and improvements. Moreover, thinking about talent from a systems efficiency standpoint emphasizes the importance of our most important resource – young people interested in participating in our sport.

Haldane goes further to say "That is the reason why I have no philosophy myself, and must be my excuse for dreaming".[218] There is much in this last statement. It encourages us to not become too dependent on a specific worldview. Science is rife with examples of when marriage to a specific model or theory interferes with forward progression in a field. In one of the more provocative articles of the past two decades, scientist and physician John Ioannidis argued that "most published research findings are false".[219] He makes this claim based on methodological limitations such as small samples and effect sizes, as well as flaws in the more social elements of how science works (e.g., researcher biases, effects of incentives/disincentives on researcher behavior).

I think you could make a similarly bold claim that "most studies of elite performers are not very useful". As noted throughout this book, research in this field has used overly simplistic designs, often from unidimensional perspectives that do not capture the complexity of the phenomenon under examination. By focusing on athletes who were successful in the past, they likely also suffer from 'cohort effects', which limits their relevance for athletes developing in a system that might be considerably different from those of the past. Most importantly, by focusing on athletes at or near the end of their development (e.g., studies of elite performers), the vast majority of work in this area suffers from 'survivorship bias'. More specifically, because this research focuses on those who emerge at the end of the athlete development process, this limits our understanding to those who were able to 'survive' the current system, not who could have survived and perhaps achieved even greater outcomes had the system been designed differently.

What is clear is that our scientific worldview is incomplete and will change in the future. This doesn't mean the answer is to stick our collective heads in the sand. This creates sporting cultures and daily training environments that allow tyrannical approaches to talent to thrive. It's important to use existing evidence to challenge the status quo. To this end, we can make some relatively firm directives based on what we know at this moment. Let's call these *Principles of Talent Development*:

Principle 1 – Individuals differ on elements related to talent.
At this point in the book, this principle shouldn't come as a surprise. The reality that people differ on all elements of function, development and performance is the basis of the 1st Law of Behavioral Genetics discussed in an earlier chapter. Sometimes these elements of talent are related to immediate performance and sometimes to factors that affect long-term development, but there is always an influence of genetic variation.

Principle 2 – Predictors of performance change across development.
The elements that explain and predict performance early in development are usually not the same as the elements that predict performance later. As a result, things that were important in child or adolescent athletes may not be as relevant later in development (e.g., due to population homogeneity, changes in performance demands).

Principle 3 - Models of athlete development and prediction need to be multi-faceted and flexible
Models of athlete development can not simply focus on performance at a specific time point in development since this performance is the end result of an enormously complicated pattern of behavior, opportunity and genetic predispositions. At the very least, models need to go beyond simply focusing on physical and technical elements of skill development and performance to include elements of psychological, cognitive and perceptual development.

Principle 4 – Predicting long-term outcomes is a bad idea… but is often necessary

Based on principles 1 to 3, it would be easy to argue sport stakeholders should never engage in long-term predictions of development or potential. However, the reality is that due to resource limitations, coaches often must make choices about who gets an opportunity and who doesn't. Recognizing that sometimes these predictions are inevitable is important. However, it is also important to acknowledge the limitations of these predictions and take steps to reduce their effects on an athlete's long-term development. At the moment, evidence suggests they are incredibly powerful.

Principle 5 – Frameworks and models built solely on the experiences of successful athletes are flawed.
The reality is that it is difficult to acquire high-quality evidence on the pathways to sporting success. As a result, those working to create evidence-based policies and practice often must 'take what they can get'. Nonetheless, it is important to remember the limitations associated with different types of research, and that an existing research base may be affected by survivor effects, cohort effects, and cognitive biases.

There are a range of things we do not currently know and it's important that we acknowledge these limitations. They highlight the gaps in understanding that future researchers will explore… and the areas of opportunity for those working in high-performance settings capable of capitalizing on them. An article in the Harvard Business Review tells the story of how British Cycling developed one of the most dominant cycling nations in history in just a few decades. The improvement emerged under the leadership of Sir Dave Brailsford, an ex-professional cyclist who took over the reins in 2002. As the article notes, Brailsford used a strategy of 'marginal gains' – "he gambled that if the team broke down everything they could think of that goes into competing on a bike, and then improved each element by 1%, they would achieve a significant aggregated increase in performance."[220]

A similar approach to the identification, selection and development of talented athletes would focus on small improvements in the reliability and validity of how athletes are assessed, developing slightly more sophisticated models of the factors affecting skill acquisition and generating marginally more accurate predictive models of development and performance outcomes. While massive improvements in any one of these elements may be unlikely due to the complexity and randomness involved, small gains in multiple areas may be possible, leading to larger overall effects.

Best-selling books would have you believe that the secret to superior performance is grit, or mindset, or time spent in deliberate practice (or a combination of the 3!). These simple explanations are appealing to a brain that seems inordinately wired to love a good dichotomy (nature vs. nurture, practice vs. play, specialization vs. sampling), but, unsurprisingly given the low rates of predictive success, we are more complex than these dichotomies suggest. For one performer, being grittier is critical, for another it's focused practice with a good teacher. The possible solutions are as varied as the athletes looking for them.

We have the potential to generate more complete answers many of the 'big' questions about athlete development, including controversial issues like when should intensive training begin for young athletes? When is too early to specialize? Can you develop positive qualities in athletes and turn them into Olympic champions? But the answers to these questions will require different approaches than we've seen in the research to date. Policy makers and coaches also seem reluctant to challenge the status quo, but knowledge waits on the other side. What is clear is that notions of talent do not have to be tyrannical or deterministic. In fact, positioning them in this way undermines what talent is, how it affects our development and performance, and our capacity to guide our own destinies.

Acknowledgements

This book would not have been possible without the help of many people. As someone who has researched talent and development for decades, I'm aware of how fortunate I am to be surrounded by a web of supportive colleagues, friends, and family, and to work in an environment that allows me to explore these types of questions with the most capable coaches, athletes, researchers, and administrators in the world.

I'd like to especially acknowledge those who reviewed some or all of the book in its various versions. These include Josh Boyd, Jack Coles, Lou Farah, Melissa Hopwood, Sean Horton, Dave and Debbie Islam, Adam Kelly, Alex McAuley, Katie Johnston, Nick Wattie, Stuart Wilson, and Sheila Winegarden. Although all errors herein are mine alone, their feedback and thoughtful criticism was invaluable. I'd also like to thank those who helped me track down information and sources, and/or provided advice on navigating the publishing system, including Ken Campbell, Jess Dixon, Rob Gray, Dave Mann and Marijke Taks.

Finally, none of this would have been possible without the love, support and endless enthusiasm of my wife, Ann-Marie. Thank you… for everything.

Joe Baker
Barrie, Canada

Author Notes

1. It's called the 2D:4D ratio and it's a predictor of how much testosterone you were exposed to *in utero*. The hypothesis here is that greater exposure increases your likelihood of success in some sports. For example, see: Baker, J., Kungl, A. M., Pabst, J., Strauss, B., Buesch, D., & Schorer, J. (2013). Your fate is in your hands? Handedness, digit ratio (2D: 4D), and selection to a national talent development system. *Laterality: Asymmetries of Body, Brain and Cognition, 18*(6), 710-718.
2. Find the amazing video here - https://www.youtube.com/watch?v=T4F9MiTeV30.
3. The process is much more complicated than I make it sound here. See https://www.psychologytoday.com/ca/articles/201001/how-win-american-idol
4. Johnson, K., Wattie, N., Schorer, J., & Baker, J. (2018). Talent identification in sport: A systematic review. *Sports Medicine, 48,* 97-109.
5. Data from Google Scholar.
6. Campbell, K. & Parcels, J. (2013). *Selling the dream: How hockey parents and their kids are paying the price for our national obsession.* Viking.
7. Calvin, M. (2017). *No hunger in paradise: The players, the journey, the dream.* Penguin.
8. https://inews.co.uk/sport/football/premier-league-academy-players-figures-appearances-numbers-1387302
9. The non-sport related odds come from: Baer, G. (2003). *Life: The odds and how to improve them.* Gotham Books & Shapiro, A., Firth Campbell, L., & Wright, R. (2014). *The book of odds: From lightning strikes to love at first sight, the odds of everyday life.* William Morrow.
10. These feelings aren't always positive. Work by Carol Dweck suggests that those who believe their feelings result from natural talent have a 'fixed mindset' which can lead to maladaptive behaviours when they experience setbacks or failure.
11. To be clear, neither the coach or scout, not anyone else in the article explicitly called this 'talent' but it was positioned as such, otherwise, the signing of the player to an elite development club doesn't make sense (i.e., why sign him if his current capacity is the result of greater practice?). https://www.bbc.com/news/av/uk-58988254

12. Cobley, S., Schorer, J. & Baker, J. (2012). Identification and development of sport talent: A brief introduction to a growing field of research and practice. In J. Baker, S. Cobley & J. Schorer (Eds.) *Talent identification and development in sport: International perspectives* (pp. 1-10). Routledge.
13. Tucker, R. (2013, November 18). *The science of sport: What is talent?* Retrieved from https://www.facebook.com/permalink.php?story_fbid=708988592445516&id=213103522034028
14. Issurin, V. B. (2017). Evidence-based prerequisites and precursors of athletic talent: A review. *Sports Medicine, 47*, 1993–2010.
15. Davids, K., Güllich, A., Shuttleworth, R., & Araujo, D. (2017). Understanding environmental and task constraints on talent development: Analysis of micro-structure of practice and macro-structure of development histories. In J. Baker, S. Cobley, J. Schorer, & N. Wattie (Eds.). *Routledge handbook of talent identification and development in sport* (pp. 192–206). London: Routledge.
16. Jones, J., Johnston, K. & Baker, J. (2020). "I can't teach you to be taller": How Canadian, collegiate level coaches construct talent in sport. *Case Studies in Sport and Exercise Psychology, 4,* 84-94. Baker, J., Wilson, S., Johnston, K., Koenigsberg, A., de Vegt, S. & Wattie, N. (2020). Talent research in sport 1990-2018: A scoping review. *Frontiers in Psychology: Performance Science, 11,* 607710
17. Sagan, C. (1995). *The demon-haunted world: Science as a candle in the dark.* Random House.
18. First recorded use was in a poem by John Lydgate a monk/poet at a priory in Essex, England. "*Bareyn of vertu, allas! who shal me save Fro feendys daunger, t'acounte for my talent?" A Selection from the Minor Poems of Dan John Lydgate* (J. O. Halliwell-Phillips, ed. 1840)
19. Tsay, C-J & Banaji, M.R. (2011). Naturals and strivers: Preferences and beliefs about sources of achievement. *Journal of Experimental Social Psychology, 47*, 460-465.
20. Not for any nefarious or superstitious reasons, simply because the extra light allowed them to travel home more safely.
21. Terman, L.M. (1917). The intelligence quotient of Francis Galton in childhood. *American Journal of Psychology, 28*, 209-215.
22. Cox, C.M. (1926). *Genetic studies of genius, volume II: The early mental traits of three hundred geniuses.* Stanford University Press.
23. Not everyone was impressed with Galton's advice. Sir Samuel Baker, another prominent African explorer, took issue with Galton's advice on fording the river: "In that very charming and useful book by Mr. Francis Galton, "The Art of Travel," advice is given for crossing a deep river, by holding to the tail of the swimming horse. In this I cannot agree; the

safety of the man is much endangered by the heels of the horse, and his security depends upon the length of the animal's tail. In rivers abounding in crocodiles, which generally follow an animal before they seize, the man hanging on to the tail of the horse is a most alluring bait, and he would certainly be taken, should one of these horrible monsters be attracted to the party. I have always found great comfort in crossing a river by simply holding to the mane, just in front of the saddle, with my left hand, with the bridle grasped as loosely as possible, so that the horse does not feel the bit; in this position, on the off side, the animal does not feel any hindrance; the man not only can direct his horse, but his presence gives it confidence, as he can speak to it coaxingly while swimming with one arm by its side. Upon landing, he at once controls the horse by the reins within his left grasp." Baker (1867). *The Nile Tributaries of Abyssinia.* I think I agree with Sir Samuel.

24. Keynes, R. (2003). *Fossils, finches, and Fuegians: Darwin's adventures and discoveries on the Beagle.* Oxford University Press.
25. Dreiskaemper, D., Strauss, B., Hagemann, N., & Büsch, D. (2013). Influence of red jersey color on physical parameters in combat sports. *Journal of Sport and Exercise Psychology*, *35*(1), 44-49. Rowe, C., Harris, J. M., & Roberts, S. C. (2005). Seeing red? Putting sportswear in context. *Nature*, *437*(7063), E10-E10.
26. Dobzhansky, T. (1973). Nothing in biology makes sense except in the light of evolution. *American Biology Teacher, 35,* 125–129,
27. Galton, F. (1869). *Hereditary genius*. Macmillan.
28. These values came from "Phillips, R. (1835). *A million of facts*. London: Darton and Clark" and Walford, E. (1862). *Men of the time: A biographical dictionary of eminent living characters (including women).* London: Boutledge, Warne & Routledge.
29. Wilson, S., Wilson, M.J., & Baker, J. (2019). Parental sport achievement and the development of athlete expertise. *European Journal of Sport Science, 17,* 511-518. Having sporting siblings also seems important see Hopwood, M.J., Farrow, D., MacMahon, C., & Baker, J. (2015). Sibling dynamics and sport expertise. *Scandinavian Journal of Medicine and Science in Sports, 25,* 724-733.
30. Okrent, D. (2019). *The guarded gate: Bigotry, eugenics, and the law that kept two generations of Jews, Italians and other European immigrants out of America.* Scribner.
31. According to an online inflation calculator, this would be around £750,000 in today's currency. https://www.in2013dollars.com/uk/inflation/1850?amount=5000
32. From review/summary of the 1914 edition of Hereditary Genius in *Eugenics Review* October 1914, pp. 251.

33. Dawkins, R. (2011). The tyranny of the discontinuous mind. The New Statesman. https://www.newstatesman.com/politics/2011/12/issue-essay-line-dawkins
34. Yoakam, C.S. & Yerkes, R.M. (1920). *Army mental tests.* H. Holt and Co: New York. Pg. 27
35. Ibid.
36. From Wikipedia - https://en.wikipedia.org/wiki/Intelligence
37. In addition to the need to screen soldiers in WWI, it's important to note that incredible changes that were occurring in healthcare during this time. Remember, it was just prior to this period that the germ theory of disease and the need for sterilization of medical instruments was occurring. All this to say, several key social systems were undergoing rapid change.
38. Interestingly, although a factor analysis might see these as independent 'factors' in our example, there is a decent base of evidence indicating cardiorespiratory fitness and cognitive functioning are related. See Chaddock, L., Hillman, C. H., Pontifex, M. B., Johnson, C. R., Raine, L. B., & Kramer, A. F. (2012). Childhood aerobic fitness predicts cognitive performance one year later. *Journal of Sports Sciences, 30*(5), 421-430.
39. There has been considerable criticism of Spearman's work, ranging from 'there are more than two factors' (e.g., the work of Cattell, R.B. (1971) *Abilities: Their structure, growth and action.* Boston, MA: Houghton Mifflin) and 'there are different factors (Gardner, H. (1999), *Intelligence reframed: Multiple intelligences for the 21st century*, Basic Books; Sternberg, R. J. (1985). *Beyond IQ: A triarchic theory of intelligence.* Cambridge University Press) to 'the factors reflect statistical artifacts with no basis in reality' (Gould, S. J. (1981). *The mismeasure of man.* New York: W. W. Norton & Company.)
40. Brace, D.K. (1927). *Measuring motor ability.* New York: A.S. Barnes and Co.
41. The Oxford Dictionary of Sport Science and Medicine defines motor ability as "A genetically defined personal characteristic or trait, such as manual dexterity and reaction time which contributes to proficiency in a number of motor skills".
42. Martin, N. C., Piek, J. P., & Hay, D. (2006). DCD and ADHD: A genetic study of their shared aetiology. *Human Movement Science, 25*(1), 110-124.
43. Drowatzky, J. N., & Zuccato, F. C. (1967). Interrelationships between selected measures of static and dynamic balance. *Research Quarterly, 38*(3), 509-510. See also Tsigilis, N., Zachopoulou, E., & Mavridis, T. H. (2001). Evaluation of the specificity of selected dynamic balance tests. *Perceptual and Motor Skills, 92*(3), 827-833. De Ste Croix, M. B., & Van Hooren, B. (2020). Sensitive periods to train general motor abilities in children and

adolescents: Do they exist? A critical appraisal. *Strength and Conditioning Journal., 42(6)*, 7-14.

44. Hands, B., McIntyre, F., & Parker, H. (2018). The general motor ability hypothesis: An old idea revisited. *Perceptual and Motor Skills, 125*(2), 213-233.
45. From McCloy, C.M & Young, N.D. (1954). *Tests and measurements in health and physical education* (3rd Edition). Appleton-Century-Crofts.
46. Fullerton, H.S. (1921). Why Babe Ruth is the greatest home-run hitter. *Popular Science Monthly, 99* (4), 19-21, 110.
47. Three of these players (Sosa, McGuire and Bonds) are controversial given their links with MLB's steroid scandal in the early 2000s.
48. It's possible Woodworth didn't even know of Ruth's visit since his graduate students Albert Johanson and Joseph Holmes conducted the testing.
49. He stopped playing seriously at the age of 29 with only periodic emergences from seclusion until his death in 2008. See Brady, F. (2011). *Endgame: Bobby Fischer's remarkable rise and fall – from America's brightest prodigy to the edge of madness*. Random House: New York.
50. Ponterotto, J. (December 14, 2010). A psychological autopsy of Bobby Fischer. *Pacific Standard*. https://psmag.com/social-justice/a-psychological-autopsy-of-bobby-fischer-25959
51. Chase, W.G. & Simon, H.A. (1973). Perception in chess. *Cognitive Psychology, 4*, 55-81.
52. de Groot, A. (1965). *Thought and choice in chess*. Mouton Publishers, The Hague, the Netherlands.
53. Djakow, Petrowski, & Rudik, (1927). *Psychologie des schachspiels* [Psychology of Chess Playing]. As cited in de Groot (1965).
54. Allard, F., & Starkes, J. L. (1980). Perception in sport: Volleyball. *Journal of Sport Psychology* 2(1), 22-33. Allard, F., Graham, S., & Paarsalu, M. E. (1980). Perception in sport: Basketball. *Journal of Sport Psychology*, 2(1), 14-21.
55. Abernethy, B., Gill, D. P., Parks, S. L., & Packer, S. T. (2001). Expertise and the perception of kinematic and situational probability information. *Perception, 30*, 233–252. Abernethy, B., & Russell, D. G. (1987). The relationship between expertise and visual-search strategy in a racquet sport. *Human Movement Science, 6*, 283–319. Abernethy, B., & Zawi, K. (2007). Pickup of essential kinematics underpins expert perception of movement patterns. *Journal of Motor Behavior, 39*, 353–367.
56. Loffing, F., Hagemann, N., & Strauss, B. (2012). Left-handedness in professional and amateur tennis. *PloS One, 7*(11), e49325.
57. Any deviation in the frequency of what a hitter sees in 'normal' situations seems to make a difference. Baseball seems well aware of this

phenomenon, as reflected in the value of 'knuckleball' pitchers; Cy Young winner, R.A. Dickey is the most successful recent example. A similar situation occurred when Major League Baseball began bringing in elite pitchers from Japan. These early pitchers had uncommon biomechanics, which made them more difficult to predict. See this example of Hideo Nomo pitching in the 1995 All Star Game - https://www.youtube.com/watch?v=aVGgtIROqPQ&t=54s

58. Quote taken from p. 402, Simon & Chase (1973).
59. Another major factor was the invention of a Morse-code reader in 1914, which could read coded transmissions automatically and at a faster rate than humanly possible.
60. Bryan, W. L., & Harter, N. (1897). Studies in the physiology and psychology of the telegraphic language. *Psychological Review, 4*(1), 27; Bryan, W. L., & Harter, N. (1899). Studies on the telegraphic language: The acquisition of a hierarchy of habits. *Psychological Review, 6*(4), 345.
61. See for example: Book, W. F. (1925). *The psychology of skill.* Gregg; Crossman, E.R.F.W. (1959). A theory of the acquisition of speed-skill. *Ergonomics, 2*, 153-166; Snoddy, G. S. (1926). Learning and stability. *Journal of Applied Psychology, 10*, 1-36.
62. Chase, W. G., & Ericsson, K. A. (1981). Skilled memory. In. J.R. Anderson (Ed.) *Cognitive skills and their acquisition* (pp. 141-189) Lawrence Erlbaum Associates.
63. Recalling the digits of pi is a favorite amongst expert memorizers. The unofficial world record (recalling 100,000 digits) is currently held by Akira Haraguchi, a retired engineer from Japan. To memorize numbers massive enough to be beyond the comprehension of the average person, and to circumvent the short-term memory limitations discussed in the previous chapter, expert memorizers use mnemonics to aid in their recall. For instance, Haraguchi reportedly converts numbers to syllables and then creates stories based on the sequence to be recalled, similar to an approach developed by Lewis Carroll (of Alice in Wonderland fame). Interest in these types of memory feats has increased considerably over the past few decades, perhaps most notable in the proliferation of 'memory sports'.
64. P. 326 in Woodworth, R.S. (1921). *Psychology: A study of mental life.* Prabhat Prakashan.
65. Baker, J., & Young, B. (2014). 20 years later: Deliberate practice and the development of expertise in sport. *International Review of Sport and Exercise Psychology, 7*, 135-157.
66. Güllich, A., Macnamara, B. N., & Hambrick, D. Z. (2021). What makes a champion? Early multidisciplinary practice, not early specialization,

predicts world-class performance. *Perspectives on Psychological Science*, 1745691620974772.

67. See Baker, J., Côté, J., & Abernethy, B. (2003). Learning from the experts: Practice activities of expert decision-makers in sport. *Research Quarterly for Exercise and Sport, 74*, 342-347. Baker, J., Côté, J., & Abernethy, B. (2003). Sport specific training, deliberate practice and the development of expertise in team ball sports. *Journal of Applied Sport Psychology, 15*, 12-25.
68. More details on the sample and methods can be found in these papers: Baker, J., Deakin, J., & Côté, J. (2005). On the utility of deliberate practice: Predicting performance in ultra-endurance triathletes from training indices. *International Journal of Sport Psychology, 36*, 225-240. Baker, J., Deakin, J., & Côté, J. (2005). Expertise in ultra-endurance triathletes: Early sport involvement, training structure, and the theory of deliberate practice. *Journal of Applied Sport Psychology, 17*, 64-78.
69. For a review see: Baker, J., Young. B.W., Tedesqui, R. & McCardle, L. (2020). New perspectives on deliberate practice and the development of sport expertise. In G. Tenenbaum and B. Eklund (Eds.). *Handbook of Sport Psychology* (4th edition).
70. Schuelke, M.; Wagner, K.R.; Stolz, L.E.; Hübner, C.; Riebel, T.; Kömen, W.; Braun, T.; Tobin, J.F.; Lee, S.-J. (2004). Myostatin mutation associated with gross muscle hypertrophy in a child. *New England Journal of Medicine, 350*, 2682-2688.
71. Rybalka, E., Timpani, C. A., Debruin, D. A., Bagaric, R. M., Campelj, D. G., & Hayes, A. (2020). The failed clinical story of myostatin inhibitors against Duchenne muscular dystrophy: exploring the biology behind the battle. *Cells, 9*, 2657; Wagner, K.R. (2020). The elusive promise of myostatin inhibition for muscular dystrophy. *Current Opinion in Neurology, 33*, 621-628.
72. Salzberg, S.L. (2018). Open questions: How many genes do we have. *BMC Biology, 16,* article number 94.
73. Pinker, S. (2004). Why nature & nurture won't go away. *Daedalus, 133*(4), 5-17.
74. International Human Genome Sequencing Consortium. (2004). Finishing the euchromatic sequence of the human genome. *Nature, 431*, 931–945.
75. Attia, J., Ioannidis, J. P. A., Thakkinstian, A., McEvoy, M., Scott, R. J., Minelli, C., Thompson, J., Infante-Rivard, C., & Guyatt, G. (2009). How to use an article about genetic association: B: Are the results of the study valid? *JAMA, 301*, 191–197. McAuley, A.B.T., Baker, J., Suraci, B., & Kelly, A.L. (2023). The influence and application of genetics in soccer. In A.L. Kelly (Ed.) *Talent identification and development in youth soccer: A guide for researchers and practitioners*. Routledge.

76. Ahmetov, I. I., Egorova, E. S., Gabdrakhmanova, L. J., & Fedotovskaya, O. N. (2016). Genes and athletic performance: An update. *Genetics and Sports*, *61*, 41-54. Pickering, C., Kiely, J., Suraci, B., & Collins, D. (2018). The magnitude of Yo-Yo test improvements following an aerobic training intervention are associated with total genotype score. *PLoS One*, *13*, e0207597; Timmons et al. (2010). Using molecular classification to predict gains in maximal aerobic capacity following endurance exercise training in humans. *Journal of Applied Physiology*, *108*, 1487-1496.
77. Cochrane, G. D., Sundman, M. H., Hall, E. E., Kostek, M. C., Patel, K., Barnes, K. P., & Ketcham, C. J. (2018). Genetics influence neurocognitive performance at baseline but not concussion history in collegiate student-athletes. *Clinical Journal of Sport Medicine*, *28*, 125-129. Ruiz-Contreras et al. (2014). Performance in working memory and attentional control is associated with the rs2180619 SNP in the CNR1 gene. *Genes, Brain and Behavior*, *13*, 173-178.
78. Gayagay, G., Yu, B., Hambly, B., Boston, T., Hahn, A. et al. (1998). Elite endurance athletes and the ACE I allele – The role of genes in athletic performance. *Human Genetics 103*, 48–50; Collins, M., Xenophontos, S.L., Cariolou, M.A., Mokone, G.G., Hudson, D.E. et al. (2004). The ACE gene and endurance performance during the South African Ironman triathlons. *Medicine and Science in Sports and Exercise, 36,* 1314–20; Montgomery, H.E., Marshall, R. Hemingway, H., Myerson, S., Clarkson, P. et al. (1998). Human gene for physical performance. *Nature, 393*, 221–22.
79. Pickering, C., & Kiely, J. (2017). ACTN3: More than just a gene for speed. *Frontiers in Physiology*, 1080.
80. Williams, A. G., & Folland, J. P. (2008). Similarity of polygenic profiles limits the potential for elite human physical performance. *The Journal of Physiology*, *586*(1), 113-121.
81. Allen et al. (2010). Hundreds of variants clustered in genomic loci and biological pathways affect human height. *Nature*, *467*, 832-838.
82. Simcoe et al. (2021). Genome-wide association study in almost 195,000 individuals identifies 50 previously unidentified genetic loci for eye color. *Science Advances*, *7*(11), eabd1239.
83. See https://twitter.com/wiringthebrain/status/1531683990637355009? for the original Twitter thread. It's possible Mitchell felt this PSA was necessary after a recent newspaper article described a CRISPR experiment that turned "fluffy hamsters into 'aggressive' mutant rage monsters". Here's a link to that article - https://metro.co.uk/2022/05/27/gene-editing-turns-fluffy-hamsters-into-aggressive-rage-monsters-16721041/

84. Some genes have been linked to reducing the injuries that come from high intensity training. See: Mokone, G.G., Schwellnus, M.P., Noakes, T.D., & Collins, M. (2006). The COL5A1 gene and Achilles tendon pathology. *Scandinavian Journal of Medicine and Science in Sport, 16*, 19–26.
85. Ridley, M. (2003). *Nature via nurture: Genes, experience, and what makes us human*. Harper Collins.
86. Davies, K. (2020). *Editing humanity: The CRISPR revolution and the new era of genome editing*. Simon and Schuster.
87. These population and participation values come from statistica.com.
88. This was the approach taken by Alex McAuley and his research team (I'm lucky enough to be part of this group) for one of his studies on elite soccer players from English academies. For more info see: McAuley, A. B., Hughes, D. C., Tsaprouni, L. G., Varley, I., Suraci, B., Baker, J., ... & Kelly, A. L. (2022). Genetic associations with personality and mental toughness profiles of English academy football players: An exploratory study. *Psychology of Sport and Exercise*, 102209.
89. Trampush, J. W., Yang, M. L. Z., Yu, J., Knowles, E., Davies, G., Liewald, D. C., ... & Lencz, T. (2017). GWAS meta-analysis reveals novel loci and genetic correlates for general cognitive function: a report from the COGENT consortium. *Molecular Psychiatry*, *22*(3), 336-345.
90. Hill, W. D., Marioni, R. E., Maghzian, O., Ritchie, S. J., Hagenaars, S. P., McIntosh, A. M., ... & Deary, I. J. (2019). A combined analysis of genetically correlated traits identifies 187 loci and a role for neurogenesis and myelination in intelligence. *Molecular Psychiatry*, *24*(2), 169-181.
91. Garfield, V. (2020). Sleep duration: A review of genome-wide association studies (GWAS) in adults from 2007 to 2020. *Sleep Medicine Reviews*, 101413.
92. For a review of studies on the genetics of personality (including GWAS) see Sanchez-Roige, S., Gray, J. C., MacKillop, J., Chen, C. H., & Palmer, A. A. (2018). The genetics of human personality. *Genes, Brain and Behavior*, *17*(3), e12439.
93. Pickering, C., & Kiely, J. (2021). The frequency of, and attitudes towards, genetic testing amongst athletes and support staff. *Performance Enhancement & Health*, *8*(4), 100184.
94. Tanisawa, K., Wang, G., Seto, J., Verdouka, I., Twycross-Lewis, R., Karanikolou, A., ... & Pitsiladis, Y. (2020). Sport and exercise genomics: The FIMS 2019 consensus statement update. *British Journal of Sports Medicine*, *54*(16), 969-975.
95. For recent discussions of this research see for example: Harden, K.P. (2021). *The genetic lottery: Why DNA matters for social equality*. Princeton University Press; Mitchell, K. (2018). *Innate: How the wiring of our brains shapes who we are*. Princeton University Press.

96. The intricacies of the thought experiment are much more complex than this, although this is generally how the paradox is described.
97. Tuttle, D. H., & Cornell, D. G. (1993). Maternal labeling of gifted children: Effects on the sibling relationship. *Exceptional Children*, *59*(5), 402-410.
98. Barreiros, A. N., & Fonseca, A. M. (2012). A retrospective analysis of Portuguese elite athletes' involvement in international competitions. *International Journal of Sports Science & Coaching*, *7*(3), 593-600; Barreiros, A., Côté, J., & Fonseca, A. M. (2014). From early to adult sport success: Analysing athletes' progression in national squads. *European Journal of Sport Science*, *14*(sup1), S178-S182.
99. Rees, T., Ingledew, D. K., & Hardy, L. (2005). Attribution in sport psychology: Seeking congruence between theory, research and practice. *Psychology of Sport and Exercise*, *6*(2), 189-204.
100. For more on attribution theory see Allen, M. S. (2012). A systematic review of content themes in sport attribution research: 1954–2011. *International Journal of Sport and Exercise Psychology*, *10*(1), 1-8; Rees, T., Ingledew, D. K., & Hardy, L. (2005). Attribution in sport psychology: Seeking congruence between theory, research and practice. *Psychology of Sport and Exercise*, *6*(2), 189-204.
101. Ntoumanis, N., & Mallett, C. J. (2014). Motivation in sport: A self-determination theory perspective. In *Routledge companion to sport and exercise psychology* (pp. 91-106). Routledge; Lonsdale, C., Hodge, K., & Rose, E. (2009). Athlete burnout in elite sport: A self-determination perspective. *Journal of Sports Sciences*, *27*(8), 785-795.
102. Collins, D., & MacNamara, Á. (2012). The rocky road to the top. *Sports Medicine*, *42*, 907-914.
103. Savage, J., Collins, D., & Cruickshank, A. (2017). Exploring traumas in the development of talent: What are they, what do they do, and what do they require? *Journal of Applied Sport Psychology*, *29*, 101-117.
104. Taleb, N. (2012). *Antifragile: Things that gain from disorder*. Random House; Lukianoff, B. & Haidt, J. (2018). *The coddling of the American mind: How good intentions and bad ideas are setting up a generation for failure*. Penguin Books.
105. For a few studies of sport conversion rates, see: Barreiros, A., Côté, J., & Fonseca, A. M. (2014). From early to adult sport success: Analysing athletes' progression in national squads. *European Journal of Sport Science, 14*, S178–S182; Yustres, I., Martín, R., Fernández, L., & González-ravé, J. M. (2017). Swimming championship finalist positions on success in international swimming competitions. *PLoS One* 12, e0187462; Yustres, I., Santos del Cerro, J., Martín, R., González-Mohíno, F., Logan, O., & González-Ravé, J. M. (2019). Influence of early specialization in world ranked swimmers and general patterns to success. *PLoS One* 14:e0218601.

106. This is undoubtedly a biased presentation of what sport provides to its participants, reflecting more recent changes in how news and social media distort perceptions of reality through their content. Negative news stories are more likely to be read (or clicked on) and in an age where viewership drives content, that matters.
107. See Ryan, R. M., & Deci, E. L. (2000). Self-determination theory and the facilitation of intrinsic motivation, social development, and well-being. *American Psychologist, 55*(1), 68-78. Bandura, A. (1997). *Self-efficacy: The exercise of control.* W.H. Freeman.
108. Hardy, L., Barlow, M., Evans, L., Rees, T., Woodman, T., & Warr, C. (2017). Great British medalists: Psychosocial biographies of super-elite and elite athletes from Olympic sports. *Progress in Brain Research, 232*, 1-119.
109. The probability of getting all 8 'yes' values is hard to calculate. If things were as simple as a coin flip (i.e., equal likelihood of one result versus another), the probability of 8 successive 'yes' values is 1/256. However, things are not equal. At different points in the development pathway, the potential to be labeled a 'yes' versus a 'no' likely changes due to shifts in the size of comparison groups, etc.
110. Dweck, C. (2006). *Mindset: The new psychology of success.* Random House.
111. Burgoyne, A. P., Hambrick, D. Z., & Macnamara, B. N. (2020). How firm are the foundations of mind-set theory? The claims appear stronger than the evidence. *Psychological Science, 31*(3), 258-267.
112. Biddle, S. J. H., Wang, C. K. J., Chatzisarantis, N. L. D., & Spray, C. M. (2003). Motivation for physical activity in young people: Entity and incremental beliefs about athletic ability. *Journal of Sports Sciences, 21,* 973–989; Spray, C. M., Wang, C. K. J., Biddle, S. J. H., Chatzisarantis, N. L. D., & Warburton, V. E. (2006). An experimental test of self-theories of ability in youth sport. *Psychology of Sport and Exercise, 7,* 255–267.
113. Ommundsen, Y. (2001a). Pupils' affective responses in physical education classes: The association of implicit theories of the nature of ability and achievement goals. *European Physical Education Review, 7,* 219–242; Ommundsen, Y. (2001b). Self-handicapping strategies in physical education classes: The influence of implicit theories of the nature of ability and achievement goal orientations. *Psychology of Sport and Exercise, 2*, 139–156.
114. Jourden, F. J., Bandura, A., & Banfield, J. T. (1991). The impact of concepts of ability on self-regulatory factors and motor skill acquisition. *Journal of Sport & Exercise Psychology, 8*, 213–226; Wulf, G., & Lewthwaite, R. (2009). Conceptions of ability affect motor learning. *Journal of Motor Behavior, 41*, 461–467.

115. Work by Dweck (2006) as well as by Wulf et al. (2013) suggest these messages can be quite subtle, possibly without the need for conscious processing. See Dweck reference noted above and Wulf, G., Lewthwaite, R., & Hooyman, A. (2013). Can ability conceptualizations alter the impact of social comparison in motor learning? *Journal of Motor Learning and Development*, *1*, 20-30.
116. Winfield was initially arrested and charged with cruelty to animals but charges were later dropped. https://www.thestar.com/news/insight/2013/08/02/the_dave_winfield_seagull_incident_vs_toronto_blue_jays_at_exhibition_stadium_30_years_later_an_oral_history.html
117. The other two athletes drafted into four professional leagues were the NFL's Mickey McCarty and NBA's George Carter, although neither McCarty nor Carter had Winfield's level of success at the professional level.
118. Jayanthi, N. A., Post, E. G., Laury, T. C., & Fabricant, P. D. (2019). Health consequences of youth sport specialization. *Journal of Athletic Training*, *54*(10), 1040-1049. Myer, G. D., Jayanthi, N., Difiori, J. P., Faigenbaum, A. D., Kiefer, A. W., Logerstedt, D., & Micheli, L. J. (2015). Sport specialization, part I: Does early sports specialization increase negative outcomes and reduce the opportunity for success in young athletes? *Sports Health*, *7*(5), 437-442.
119. Côté, J., Lidor, R., & Hackfort, D. (2009). ISSP position stand: To sample or to specialize? Seven postulates about youth sport activities that lead to continued participation and elite performance. *International Journal of Sport and Exercise Psychology*, *7*, 7-17.
120. For a review of this scant research see - Baker, J., Cobley, S., & Fraser-Thomas, J. (2009). What do we know about early sport specialization? Not much! *High Ability Studies*, *20*, 77-89.
121. Uhls, Y. T., Ellison, N. B., & Subrahmanyam, K. (2017). Benefits and costs of social media in adolescence. *Pediatrics*, *140*(Supplement 2), S67-S70. Oswald, T. K., Rumbold, A. R., Kedzior, S. G., & Moore, V. M. (2020). Psychological impacts of "screen time" and "green time" for children and adolescents: A systematic scoping review. *PloS One*, *15*(9), e0237725.
122. Baker, J., Schorer, J., & Wattie, N. (2018). Compromising talent: Issues in identifying and selecting talent in sport. *Quest*, *70*, 48-63; Beamish, R. (1990). The persistence of inequality: An analysis of participation patterns among Canada's high performance athletes. *International Review for Sociology of Sport*, *25*, 143-152.
123. Hofferth, S. L., & Sandberg, J. F. (2001). Changes in American children's time, 1981–1997. *Advances in Life Course Research*, *6*, 193-229. Hofferth, S.

L. (2009). Changes in American children's time–1997 to 2003. *Electronic International Journal of Time Use Research, 6*, 26. Sandberg, J. F., & Hofferth, S. L. (2001). Changes in children's time with parents: United States, 1981–1997. *Demography, 38*, 423-436.

124. Abi-Jaoude, E., Naylor, K. T., & Pignatiello, A. (2020). Smartphones, social media use and youth mental health. *CMAJ, 192*(6), E136-E141. Riehm et al. (2019). Associations between time spent using social media and internalizing and externalizing problems among US youth. *JAMA Psychiatry, 76*(12), 1266-1273.
125. Ericsson, K. A., Krampe, R. T., & Tesch-Römer, C. (1993). The role of deliberate practice in the acquisition of expert performance. *Psychological Review, 100*, 363-406. (pp. 391).
126. In an edition of his excellent 'Range Report' (https://davidepstein.bulletin.com/even-tiger-and-mozart-weren-t-tiger-and-mozart), David Epstein noted that even Tiger participated in different sports as a youth, questioning the validity of this 'specialization narrative'. This likely reflects the lack of precision we have in determining what 'specialization' means rather than de-throning Tiger as the King of Specialization. It also reinforces an emerging trend that sport specialization may not be as prevalent as the rhetoric suggests.
127. Social determinants of health include the nonmedicinal factors that influence our health and development. The most common and influential factors are measures of socioeconomic status such as income and employment, and indicators of environmental quality (e.g., safety, security).
128. Khalil, K., Hopwood, M., Farrow, D., MacMahon, C., & Baker, J. (October 2014). Socioeconomic factors in high performance athlete development. Paper presented at the 2014 Conference of the *Canadian Society for Psychomotor Learning and Sport Psychology*, London, Canada.
129. Fiskerstrand, A. & Seiler, K.S. (2004). Training and performance characteristics among Norwegian International Rowers 1970–2001. *Scandinavian Journal of Medicine and Science in Sports, 13*, 303-310.
130. Orie et al. (2014). Thirty-eight years of training distribution in Olympic speed skaters. *International Journal of Sport Physiology and Performance, 9*, 93-99.
131. Campbell, K. & Parcels, J. (2013). *Selling the dream: How hockey parents and their kids are paying the price for our national obsession.* Viking.
132. For an excellent discussion of the research in this area, see Hutchison, A. (2018). *Endure: Mind, body and curiously elastic limits of human performance*. Harper Collins.
133. Thorndike E L (1923). *Educational psychology: Briefer course.* Columbia University Press. Thorndike E L (1923). The influence of first year Latin upon the ability to read English. *School Sociology 17*, 165-168. Woodworth,

R. S., & Thorndike, E. L. (1901). The influence of improvement in one mental function upon the efficiency of other functions.(I). *Psychological Review*, *8*(3), 247.

134. Flynn, M. G., Carroll, K. K., Hall, H. L., Bushman, B. A., Brolinson, P. G., & Weideman, C. A. (1998). Cross training: Indices of training stress and performance. *Medicine and Science in Sports and Exercise*, *30*(2), 294-300. Foster, C., Hector, L. L., Welsh, R., Schrager, M., Green, M. A., & Snyder, A. C. (1995). Effects of specific versus cross-training on running performance. *European Journal of Applied Physiology and Occupational Physiology*, *70*(4), 367-372. Millet, G. P., Candau, R. B., Barbier, B., Busso, T., Rouillon, J. D., & Chatard, J. C. (2002). Modelling the transfers of training effects on performance in elite triathletes. *International Journal of Sports Medicine*, *23*(01), 55-63. Mutton, D. L., Loy, S. F., Rogers, D. M., Holland, G. J., Vincent, W. J., & Heng, M. I. N. G. (1993). Effect of run vs combined cycle/run training on VO2max and running performance. *Medicine and Science in Sports and Exercise*, *25*(12), 1393-1397.
135. Fraser-Thomas, J. L., Côté, J., & Deakin, J. (2005). Youth sport programs: An avenue to foster positive youth development. *Physical Education & Sport Pedagogy*, *10*(1), 19-40. Turnnidge, J., Côté, J., & Hancock, D. J. (2014). Positive youth development from sport to life: Explicit or implicit transfer? *Quest*, *66*(2), 203-217.
136. Loy, S. F., Hoffmann, J. J., & Holland, G. J. (1995). Benefits and practical use of cross-training in sports. *Sports Medicine*, *19*, 1-8. Rowell, L. B. (1986). *Human circulation: Regulation during physical stress*. Oxford University Press. Saltin, B., Nazar, K., Costill, D. L., Stein, E., Jansson, E., Essén, B., & Gollnick, P. D. (1976). The nature of the training response: Peripheral and central adaptations to one-legged exercise. *Acta Physiologica Scandinavica*, *96*, 289-305. Sutton, J. R. (1992). Limitations to maximal oxygen uptake. *Sports Medicine*, *13*, 127-133.
137. Crane, J., & Temple, V. (2015). A systematic review of dropout from organized sport among children and youth. *European Physical Education Review*, *21*(1), 114-131.
138. Mol, S. E., & Bus, A. G. (2011). To read or not to read: A meta-analysis of print exposure from infancy to early adulthood. *Psychological Bulletin*, *137*(2), 267. d'Apice, K., Latham, R. M., & von Stumm, S. (2019). A naturalistic home observational approach to children's language, cognition, and behavior. *Developmental Psychology*, *55*(7), 1414.
139. Rigney, D. (2010). *The Matthew effect: How advantage begets further advantage*. Columbia University Press.
140. Also known as the community size effect. See Baker, J., Shuiskiy, K., & Schorer, J. (2014). Does size of one's community affect likelihood of being drafted into the NHL? Analysis of 25 years of data. *Journal of Sports*

Sciences, 32(16), 1570-1575; Wattie, N., Schorer, J., & Baker, J. (2018). Seeing the forest but not the trees: Heterogeneity in community size effects in Canadian ice hockey players. *Journal of Sports Sciences, 36*(4), 436-444.

141. de Groot, R., van den Hurk, K., Schoonmade, L. J., de Kort, W. L., Brug, J., & Lakerveld, J. (2019). Urban-rural differences in the association between blood lipids and characteristics of the built environment: A systematic review and meta-analysis. *BMJ Global Health, 4*(1); Johnson III, J. A., & Johnson, A. M. (2015). Urban-rural differences in childhood and adolescent obesity in the United States: A systematic review and meta-analysis. *Childhood Obesity, 11*(3), 233-241; Purtle, J., Nelson, K. L., Yang, Y., Langellier, B., Stankov, I., & Roux, A. V. D. (2019). Urban–rural differences in older adult depression: A systematic review and meta-analysis of comparative studies. *American Journal of Preventive Medicine, 56*(4), 603-613.
142. Doyle, A. C. (1888). On the geographical distribution of British intellect. *The Nineteenth century and after: A monthly review, 24*(138), 184-195.
143. Lodge, H. C. (1891). The distribution of ability in the United States. *Century Magazine, 42*, 687-694. The balance, eloquence and curiosity of Conan Doyle's approach was sorely missing from Lodge's piece, likely due to his well known background as a prominent eugenicist and proponent of immigration reform in the US. In Lodge's report, race is a clear focus. For more on Henry Cabot Lodge and his views on race, immigration, intellect and social value see Okrent, D. (2019). *The guarded gate: Bigotry, eugenics, and the law that kept two generations of Jews, Italians, and other European immigrants out of America.* Scribner.
144. Côté, J., MacDonald, D., Baker, J., & Abernethy, B. (2006). When "where" is more important than "when": Birth place effects on the achievement of sporting expertise. *Journal of Sports Sciences, 24*, 1065-1073.
145. Rossing, N. N., Stentoft, D., Flattum, A., Côté, J., & Karbing, D. S. (2018). Influence of population size, density, and proximity to talent clubs on the likelihood of becoming elite youth athlete. *Scandinavian Journal of Medicine & Science in Sports, 28*(3), 1304-1313.
146. Gladwell, M. (2007). *Outliers: The story of success.* Little, Brown and Co; Levitt, S. & Dubner, S. (2009). *Superfreaknomics: Global cooling patriotic prostitutes, and why suicide bombers should buy life insurance.* William Morrow.
147. Schorer, J., Wattie, N., & Baker, J. R. (2013). A new dimension to relative age effects: Constant year effects in German youth handball. *PloS One, 8*(4), e60336.
148. This approach is also used in education when school boards and municipalities use a cutoff date to place children into grades. As a result, relative age effects are also common in these settings. See for instance

Cobley, S. McKenna, J., Baker, J., & Wattie, N. (2009). How pervasive are relative age effects in secondary school education? *Journal of Educational Psychology, 101,* 520-528.

149. Baker, J., & Logan, A. J. (2007). Developmental contexts and sporting success: Birth date and birthplace effects in national hockey league draftees 2000–2005. *British Journal of Sports Medicine, 41*(8), 515-517; Kelly, A. L., Jackson, D. T., Barrell, D., Burke, K., & Baker, J. (2021). Relative age effects in international rugby union: Consequences of changing the cutoff date and exploring youth to senior transitions. *High Ability Studies*, 1-20; Romann, M., & Fuchslocher, J. (2013). Relative age effects in Swiss junior soccer and their relationship with playing position. *European Journal of Sport Science, 13*(4), 356-363; Till, K., Cobley, S., Wattie, N., O'hara, J., Cooke, C., & Chapman, C. (2010). The prevalence, influential factors and mechanisms of relative age effects in UK Rugby League. *Scandinavian Journal of Medicine & Science in Sports, 20*(2), 320-329.
150. Helsen, W. F., Baker, J., Michiels, S., Schorer, J., Van Winckel, J., & Williams, A. M. (2012). The relative age effect in European professional soccer: Did ten years of research make any difference? *Journal of Sports Sciences, 30*(15), 1665-1671. Webdale, K., Baker, J., Schorer, J., & Wattie, N. (2020). Solving sport's 'relative age' problem: A systematic review of proposed solutions. *International Review of Sport and Exercise Psychology*, *13*(1), 187-204.
151. Ashworth J, Heyndels B. (2007). Selection bias and peer effects in team sports: The effect of age grouping on earnings of German soccer players. *Journal of Sports Economics, 8,* 355–377. Baker, J., & Logan, A.J. (2007). Developmental contexts and sporting success: Birth date and birthplace effects in national hockey league draftees 2000–2005. *British Journal of Sports Medicine, 41,*515–517. Schorer, J., Cobley, S., Büsch, D., Bräutigam, H., & Baker, J. (2009). Influences of competition level, gender, player nationality, career stage and playing position on relative age effects. *Scandinavian Journal of Medicine & Science in Sports*, *19*(5), 720-730. Steingröver, C., Wattie, N., Baker, J., & Schorer, J. (2016). Does relative age affect career length in North American professional sports? *Sports Medicine-Open*, *2*(1), 1-7.
152. https://www.espn.com/espn/feature/story/_/id/16425548/michael-phelps-prepares-life-2016-rio-olympics
153. https://www.bloomberg.com/news/features/2015-08-28/costs-of-noah-rubin-becoming-the-world-s-631st-best-tennis-player
154. Campbell, K. & Parcels, J. (2013). *Selling the dream: How hockey parents and their kids are paying the price for our national obsession.* Viking.

155. Assuming 8 hours per day for sleep and 2 hours for eating and other necessities of life (showering, going to the bathroom, brushing teeth, etc), it would take 714 days to accumulate 10,000 hours of practice.
156. Hopwood, M., MacMahon, C., Farrow, D., & Baker, J. (2015). Is practice the only determinant of sporting expertise? Revisiting Starkes (2000). *International Journal of Sport Psychology, 46.*
157. Carlson, K., Kim, J., Lusardi, A., & Camerer, C.F. (2015). Bankruptcy rates among NFL players with short-lived income spikes. https://www.nber.org/papers/w21085
158. Cooper, D. J., Batt, M. E., O'Hanlon, M. S., & Palmer, D. (2021). A cross-sectional study of retired great British Olympians (Berlin 1936-Sochi 2014): Olympic career injuries, joint health in later life, and reasons for retirement from Olympic sport. *Sports Medicine: Open, 7.* 54.
159. Kontro, T. K., Sarna, S., Kaprio, J., & Kujala, U. M. (2018). Mortality and health-related habits in 900 Finnish former elite athletes and their brothers. *British Journal of Sports Medicine, 52*(2), 89-95.
160. Lemez, S. & Baker, J. (2015). Do elite athletes live longer: A systematic review of mortality and longevity in elite athletes. *Sports Medicine – Open, 1,* 15.
161. Baker, J., Koz, D., Kungl, A. M., Fraser-Thomas, J., & Schorer, J. (2013). Staying at the top: Playing position and performance affect career length in professional sport. *High Ability Studies*, *24*(1), 63-76.
162. This quote comes from: Duckworth, A. (2016). *Grit: The power of passion and perseverance.* Scribner. In this book, the author provides a very rich and interesting discussion of how elite performers view this type of dedication.
163. https://www.ccmhs-ccsms.ca/
164. Massey, C., & Thaler, R. H. (2013). The loser's curse: Decision making and market efficiency in the National Football League draft. *Management Science, 59*, 1479-1495.
165. This obviously does not include the potential mountains of proprietary research done by professional teams that remains 'in house'.
166. This isn't exactly true; there was some stability in the last rounds of the draft as well, but in a negative direction. Johnston, K., Farah, L., Ghuman, H., & Baker, J. (2021). To draft or not to draft? A systematic review of North American sports' entry draft. *Scandinavian Journal of Medicine and Science in Sports.*
167. For popular summaries of their research see: Gigerenzer, G. (2003). *Reckoning with risk: Learning to live with uncertainty*. Penguin. Kahnemann, D. (2013). *Thinking, fast and slow.* Farrar, Straus and Giroux. Tetlock, P.E. & Gardner, D (2016). *Superforecasting: The art and science of prediction.* Random House.

168. See Farah, L. & Baker, J. (2021). Eliminating buyer's remorse: An examination of the sunk cost fallacy in the National Hockey League draft. *Scandinavian Journal of Medicine and Science in Sports, 31,* 1363-1370. Keefer, Q. A. (2019). Decision-maker beliefs and the sunk-cost fallacy: Major League Baseball's final-offer salary arbitration and utilization. *Journal of Economic Psychology*, *75*, 102080. Keefer, Q.A.W. (2015). Performance feedback does not eliminate the sunk-cost fallacy: Evidence from professional football. *Journal of Labor Research, 36*, 409-426; Staw, B.M. & Hoang, H. (1995). Sunk costs in the NBA: Why draft order affects playing time and survival in professional basketball. *Administrative Science Quarterly*, 40(3), 474-494.
169. The quote is from - Posnanski, J. (2010). It gets more hype than ever, but the NFL draft is still a crapshoot. *Sports Illustrated*, https://www.si.com/more-sports/2010/04/22/draft-history
170. Lyons, B. D., Hoffman, B. J., & Michel, J. W. (2009). Not much more than g? An examination of the impact of intelligence on NFL performance. *Human Performance*, *22*(3), 225-245; Pitts, J. D., & Evans, B. (2018). Evidence on the importance of cognitive ability tests for NFL quarterbacks: What are the relationships among Wonderlic scores, draft positions and NFL performance outcomes? *Applied Economics*, *50*(27), 2957-2966.
171. Mamula has the second highest Wonderlic score of NFL players ever. He's only beaten by Pan McInally, a punter drafted by the Cincinnati Bengals in 1975.
172. This isn't to say there's no interest in cognition. The research in this area with NFL players almost exclusively looks at the effects of playing football generally, or amount of physical contact in particular, on cognitive functioning after their career ends. The evidence is not promising.
173. For a recent review of work in this area see Hodges, N.J., Wyder-Hodge, P.A., Hetherington, S., Baker, J., Besler, Z., & Spering, M. (2021). Topical Review: Perceptual-cognitive skills, methods, and skill-based comparisons in interceptive sports. *Optometry and Vision Science*, *98*(7), 681-695.
174. The actual quote by Einstein is less elegant but the point remains the same - "the supreme goal of all theory is to make the irreducible basic elements as simple and as few as possible without having to surrender the adequate representation of a single datum of experience".
175. The term 'antique ignorances' comes from a series of lectures by psychologist Daniel Robinson as part of the Great Courses series. In his lecture on the legal and philosophical basis for the insanity defense, Robinson summarizes the argument made by Thomas Erskine in the 19th century in the trial of James Hatfield, an ex-soldier who attempted to kill

King George III. By all accounts, Erskine was a brilliant lawyer; in this case, he summarized English legal precedent on the criteria for insanity before dismantling the argument as no longer reflective of what the knowledge of the day said about the human mind and brain. In describing Erskine's argument to the jury, Robinson noted Erskine urged the jury to not be held hostage by 'antique ignorances' but it is unclear whether this term is Erskine's or Robinson's. Regardless, it is a fascinating term and fits well with the context of sport, where many obviously ill-suited and disproven things still occur because 'that's the way it's always been done'. Here's a link to a transcript of Robinson's lecture - https://www.thegreatcoursesdaily.com/insanity-defense/

176. Other (potentially more significant) forces include capitalistic notions of every sport for itself, and the billion dollar industry of elite youth sport.
177. Baker, J., Wattie, N. & Schorer, J. (2019). A proposed conceptualization of talent in sport: The first step in a long and winding road. *Psychology of Sport and Exercise, 43*, 27-33.
178. Howe, M. J. A., Davidson, J. W., & Sloboda, J. A. (1998). Innate talents: Reality or myth? *Behavioral and Brain Sciences, 21*, 399–442.
179. Gagné, F. (2004). Transforming gifts into talents: The DMGT as a developmental theory. *High Ability Studies, 15*, 119–147
180. This definition of 'innate' is too simple since we know environmental influences do not start a birth and individuals are highly affected by their mother's gestational environment.
181. Lykken, D. T. (1982). Research with twins: The concept of emergenesis. *Psychophysiology, 19*, 361–373; Lykken, D. T. (2006). The mechanism of emergenesis. *Genes, Brain and Behavior, 5*, 306–310; Lykken, D. T., McGue, M., Tellegen, A., & Bouchard, T. J., Jr. (1992). Emergenesis: Genetics traits may not run in families. *American Psychologist, 47*, 1565–1577
182. See for example, Keller, M. C., Coventry, W. I., Health, A. C., & Martin, N. G. (2005). Widespread evidence of non-additive genetic variation in Cloninger's and Eysenck's personality dimensions using a twin plus sibling design. *Behavior Genetics, 35*, 707–721. Lykken, D. T., Bouchard, T. J., Jr., McGue, M., & Tellegen, A. (1993). The heritability of interests: A twin study. *Journal of Applied Psychology, 78*, 649–661. Simonton, D. K. (2003). Expertise, competence, and creative ability. In R. Sternberg, & E. Grigorenko (Eds.). *The psychology of abilities, competencies, and expertise* (pp. 213– 240). Cambridge University Press. Simonton, D. K. (2009). *Genius 101*. Springer.
183. Allen, H. L., Estrada, K., Lettre, G., et al. (2010). Hundreds of variants clustered in genomic loci and biological pathways affect human height. *Nature, 467*, 832–838.

184. Sapolsky, R.M. (2017). *Behave: The biology of humans at our best and worst.* Penguin.

185. Davids, K., & Baker, J. (2007). Genes, environment and sport performance: Why the nature-nurture dualism is no longer relevant. *Sports Medicine, 37*, 961–980.

186. Baker, J., Wattie, N. & Schorer, J. (2019). A proposed conceptualization of talent in sport: The first step in a long and winding road. *Psychology of Sport and Exercise, 43*, 27-33.

187. Norton, K., & Olds, T. (2001). Morphological evolution of athletes over the 20th century: Causes and consequences. *Sports Medicine, 31*, 763–783.

188. McLaughlin writes about the beginning of his journey here - *http://thedanplan.com/bouncing-back-a-return-to-australia/*

189. Phillips, S. (2017). The Average Guy Who Spent 6,003 Hours Trying to Be a Professional Golfer. *The Atlantic* *https://www.theatlantic.com/health/archive/2017/08/the-dan-plan/536592/*

190. See Piedmont, R. L., Hill, D. C., & Blanco, S. (1999). Predicting athletic performance using the five-factor model of personality. *Personality and Individual Differences, 27*(4), 769-777. Tedesqui, R. A., & Young, B. W. (2018). Comparing the contribution of conscientiousness, self-control, and grit to key criteria of sport expertise development. *Psychology of Sport and Exercise, 34*, 110-118.

191. Tedesqui, R. A., & Young, B. W. (2017). Associations between self-control, practice, and skill level in sport expertise development. *Research Quarterly for Exercise and Sport, 88*(1), 108-113.

192. McCardle, L., Young, B.W. & Baker, J. (2019) Self-regulated learning and expertise development in sport: Current status, challenges, and future opportunities, *International Review of Sport and Exercise Psychology, 12*, 1, 112-138.

193. Jonker, L., Elferink-Gemser, M. T., de Roos, I. M., & Visscher, C. (2012). The role of reflection in sport expertise. *The Sport Psychologist, 26*(2), 224-242.

194. The British Columbia governments established initiatives around the Vancouver Winter Olympics to improve the physical activity participation of this province's population by 20%. The initiatives did not seem to be successful on increasing general forms of physical activity. See for example, Craig, C. L., & Bauman, A. E. (2014). The impact of the Vancouver Winter Olympics on population level physical activity and sport participation among Canadian children and adolescents: Population based study. *International Journal of Behavioral Nutrition and Physical Activity, 11*(1), 1-9.

195. Andriessen, K., & Krysinska, K. (2009). Can sports events affect suicidal behavior? A review of the literature and implications for

prevention. *Crisis, 30*(3), 144-152. Bozsonyi, K., Osvath, P., Fekete, S., & Bálint, L. (2015). The effects of significant international sports events on Hungarian suicide rates. *Crisis, 37,* 148-154.

196. Williams, D J & Neville , F G (2014). Sport-related domestic violence: Exploring the complex relationship between sporting events and domestic violence. In MF Taylor, JA Pooley & RS Taylor (eds) *Overcoming domestic violence: Creating a dialogue around vulnerable populations* (pp. 241-258) Nova Science Publishers.
197. For a review see: Furnham, A., Richards, S. C., & Paulhus, D. L. (2013). The Dark Triad of personality: A 10 year review. *Social and Personality Psychology Compass, 7*(3), 199-216.
198. Basterfield, L., Adamson, A. J., Frary, J. K., Parkinson, K. N., Pearce, M. S., Reilly, J. J., & Gateshead Millennium Study Core Team. (2011). Longitudinal study of physical activity and sedentary behavior in children. *Pediatrics, 127*(1), e24-e30; Gordon-Larsen, P., Nelson, M. C., & Popkin, B. M. (2004). Longitudinal physical activity and sedentary behavior trends: Adolescence to adulthood. *American Journal of Preventive Medicine, 27*(4), 277-283.
199. Gould, D., Dieffenbach, K., & Moffett, A. (2002). Psychological characteristics and their development in Olympic champions. *Journal of Applied Sport Psychology, 14*(3), 172-204.
200. MacArthur, R. & Wilson, E.O. (1967). *The theory of island biogeography.* Princeton University Press
201. Although this distinction is still discussed in evolutionary science, it has been considerably expanded from Wilson and MacArthur's original work. The most recent framework for understanding growth, survival and evolution of a species is Life History Evolution. Flatt, T., & Heyland, A. (Eds.). (2011). *Mechanisms of life history evolution: The genetics and physiology of life history traits and trade-offs.* Oxford University Press.
202. This pyramid is widely discussed in sport policy. This version of the pyramid is a slight modification of the version presented by: Gulbin, J. P., Oldenziel, K. E., Weissensteiner, J. R., & Gagné, F. (2010). A look through the rear view mirror: Developmental experiences and insights of high performance athletes. *Talent Development & Excellence, 2*(2), 149-164.
203. Cobley, S., Abbott, S., Eisenhuth, J., Salter, J., McGregor, D., & Romann, M. (2019). Removing relative age effects from youth swimming: The development and testing of corrective adjustment procedures. *Journal of Science and Medicine in Sport, 22*(6), 735-740. Romann, M., & Cobley, S. (2015). Relative age effects in athletic sprinting and corrective adjustments as a solution for their removal. *PLoS One, 10*(4), e0122988.
204. This is not quite as simple as it sounds. For a discussion of implications, see: Johnston, K., Farah, L., & Baker, J. (2021). Storm clouds on the

horizon: On the emerging need to tighten selection policies. *Frontiers in Sports and Active Living*. https://www.frontiersin.org/articles/10.3389/fspor.2021.772181/full

205. Sichting, F., Kram, N. C., & Legerlotz, K. (2022). An identical twin study on human Achilles tendon adaptation: Regular recreational exercise at comparatively low intensities can increase tendon stiffness. *Frontiers in Physiology*, 2447.
206. Rottensteiner, M., Leskinen, T., Niskanen, E., Aaltonen, S., Mutikainen, S., Wikgren, J., ... & Kujala, U. M. (2015). Physical activity, fitness, glucose homeostasis, and brain morphology in twins. *Medicine and Science in Sports and Exercise, 47*(3), 509-518.
207. Huppertz, C., Bartels, M., Jansen, I. E., Boomsma, D. I., Willemsen, G., de Moor, M. H., & de Geus, E. J. (2014). A twin-sibling study on the relationship between exercise attitudes and exercise behavior. *Behavior Genetics, 44*(1), 45-55.
208. MacKinnon, J.B. (2016). The strange brain of the world's greatest solo climber. *Nautilus, 39*. https://nautil.us/issue/39/sport/the-strange-brain-of-the-worlds-greatest-solo-climber
209. Penke, L., Denissen, J. J., & Miller, G. F. (2007). The evolutionary genetics of personality. *European Journal of Personality, 21*(5), 549–587.
210. Baker, J., Johnston, K. & Wattie, N. (2022). Survival versus attraction advantages and talent selection in sport. *Sports Medicine: Open, 8,* 17.
211. Baker, J., Wattie, N., & Schorer, J. (2015). Defining expertise: A taxonomy for researchers in skill acquisition and expertise. In J. Baker and D. Farrow (Eds.) *Routledge handbook of sport expertise* (pp. 145-155). Routledge.
212. Côté, J., & Vierimaa, M. (2014). The developmental model of sport participation: 15 years after its first conceptualization. *Science & Sports, 29*, S63-S69.
213. Baker, J., Mosher, A., & Fraser-Thomas, J. (2021). Is it too early to condemn early sport specialisation? *British Journal of Sports Medicine, 55*(3), 179-180; Mosher, A., Till, K., Fraser-Thomas, J., & Baker, J. (2022). Revisiting early sport specialization: What's the problem? *Sports Health, 14*(1), 13-19.
214. These are not archetypes in the sense proposed by psychologist Carl Jung, which are grounded in universal meaning and symbols that are thought to reflect a common collective unconscious; instead, these reflect common developmental trajectories athletes may take to the top.
215. Pinker, S. (1997). *How the mind works*. W.W. Norton and Co.
216. More on Krauss' podcast can be found at www.originsprojectfoundation.org/podcast/
217. Dobzhansky, T. (1962). Genetics and equality. *Science, 137*, 112-115.

218. Haldane, J.D.S. (1927). *Possible worlds and other essays.* Chatto and Windus.
219. Ioannidis, J. (2005). Why most published research findings are false. *PLOS Medicine, 2*, e124. https://journals.plos.org/plosmedicine/article?id=10.1371/journal.pmed.0020124
220. Harrell, E. J. H. B. R. (2015). How 1% performance improvements led to Olympic gold. *Harvard Business Review, 30.*

Index

Printed in Great Britain
by Amazon

44820611R00136